THE LIFE

NICHOLAI VELIMIROVICH

THE LIFE OF ST SAVA

with an introduction
by
VESELIN KESICH

SAINT VLADIMIR'S SEMINARY PRESS
Crestwood, New York 10707
1989

Originally published in 1951 by the
Serbian Eastern Orthodox Diocese.
This edition published by permission of
Bishop Firmilian, Administrator of the former
American-Canadian Diocese of the Serbian Orthodox Church

Velimirović, Nikolaj, 1880-1956.
      The life of St. Sava / Nicholai Velimirovich ; with an
introduction by Veselin Kesich.
        p.   cm.
   Bibliography: p.
   ISBN 0-88141-065-9 : $9.95
   1. Sava, Saint, 1169-1237. 2. Christian saints--Yugoslavia--
Serbia--Biography. 3.Serbia--Biography. 4. Srpska pravoslavna
crkva--Bishops--Biography. 5. Orthodox Eastern Church-- Yugoslavia--Serbia--Bishops--
Biography. I. Title.
   BX719.S35V44 1988
   281.9'092'4--dc19
   [B]   88-24021
                                           CIP

THE LIFE OF ST SAVA

PRINTED IN THE UNITED STATES OF AMERICA
by
J & J Printing, Inc.
Syracuse, New York

Table of Contents

VI

PREFACE

This book, published in 1951 only in English, has been out of print for a number of years. In preparing the present edition, the language has been thoroughly revised and the spelling normalized to present international usage. The editors intend to preserve the spirit and expressiveness of the author and to make the book more accessible to the reader. This edition was prepared by Lydia W. Kesich. Fr Joseph Frawley provided helpful comments and the reading of the galleys. Finally, the printing of this edition could not have been achieved without the support, encouragement and blessing of Bishop Firmilian of the Serbian Orthodox Church.

Pronunciation table:

č, ć	ch
š	sh
ž	like 's' is pleasure, Asia
j	y like yes, boy
c	ts

INTRODUCTION

THE LIFE OF ST SAVA is an account of an unusual saint, written by an unusual bishop. The saint is Sava, founder and patron of the Serbian Orthodox church, and the author is Bishop Nicholai Velimirovich (1880-1956). The lives of both men are vital parts of the history of the Serbian Orthodox Church. Our purpose here is to explain to the general reader who these great churchmen are. We shall give particular attention to Bishop Nicholai's life and his contribution to the church.

St Sava

St Sava (1173-1236) is the best known and most loved of the Serbian saints. The youngest son of the Grand Župan Nemanja, the founder of the Serbian state, he left his father's home at eighteen, lived an ascetic life on Mount Athos, transformed the abandoned monastery, Hilandar, into a lasting and still flourishing center of Orthodox spirituality, wrote the first original literary work in Serbian (the life of his father, St Simeon, and became the first archbishop of the newly organized autocephalous Serbian Church in 1219.

In organizing the Serbian church, as Bishop Nicholai notes, Sava was not cutting his people off from the existing Orthodox churches. He wanted instead to make the Serbian people "worthy members of the universal Orthodox family of Christ." In his engaging account, Bishop Nicholai emphasizes that St Sava, who dedicated his life to his people as well as to his church, "felt at home in every Orthodox community, of every race and language."

This book was not intended to be primarily an historical account. In addition Bishop Nicholai conveys how the saint's life and times have been received and preserved in the memory of his people. It is also deeply personal; it was published, only in English, near the end of Bishop Nicholai's life. Undoubtedly

he had lived with his subject for many years, and the work was
the product of a long period of meditation and prayer.

In Mileševo, where St Sava was buried, there is a portrait of
St Sava which is nearly contemporary with him. Like this
book, the portrait manages to convey the personality of a
Christian saint whose life was shaped by prayer and concern
for others, who was at the same time meek and strong. This
strong and active church leader lived constantly with the words
of Jesus that "blessed are the meek." We may say that for him
this meant that those who do not make claims for themselves,
those who do not compare themselves, those who do not compare themselves with others but only with Christ, are blessed.
Both portraits suggest that Sava's strength was paradoxically
rooted in meekness. He took drastic risks for the sake of his
people and their national and spiritual survival. He is reported
to have said to his contemporaries: "I do not ask anything
from you—I desire the salvation of your souls and for the sake
of your salvation I disregard my own soul."

While demonstrating Sava's decisive leadership, Bishop
Nicholai portrays Sava as a man of deep feeling and compas-
sion. He stresses Sava's grief — as Sava himself did — at his
father's death, then his gratitude for the holiness of his end.
We may see many places in the book where Bishop Nicholai
stresses the deep emotions that Sava displayed throughout the
events of his life; we sense here the author's own engagement
with his subject.

St Sava's importance extends far beyond his considerable
achievements even within his own lifetime. Three and a half
centuries after his death, when his subject people were living
under Turkish rule, his influence grew and flourished. Muslims
as well as Christians living in the region where the saint was
buried would honor him and believed increasingly in his
miraculous power. Out of fear of the influence of this growing
cult, the rulers burned St Sava's body on Vračar in 1595. To
the veneration of a great saint and consecrated leader was add-

ed that of the martyr, and the memory of St Sava persisted and
grew among his people. This book records not only the deeds
of St Sava but this living memory, handed down within
families and communities from generation to generation,
weaving history with sacred stories.

In St Sava the Serbian people found a truly great expression
of their historical destiny as a nation. Through the centuries his
people have looked to him to know the meaning of their past
and their destiny. His greatness was recognized during his life
and even more clearly after his death. The cult of St Sava arose
among the Serbian people as a spontaneous response of a people to their shepherd. They sensed that through his achievement they had emerged as a spirtually unified entity. And yet
any great Christian leader must go beyond the boundaries of
his nation, of his local church, and enter into the history of
other nations and other local churches. St Sava belongs to the
history of Orthodox Christianity as a whole. As he brought his
people into the universal church, so the church has recognized
his universality. His cult was established in Bulgaria, Russia,
and Rumania. Particularly in this century, with the dispersal of
large numbers of Serbian Orthodox throughout the world,
especially to English-speaking countries, St Sava's name has
spread and many churches are dedicated to him. With the help
of those who keep his memory, a memorial church is now finally being built to him on Vračar, where his body was destroyed.

Perhaps his most attractive trait for our century was his
refusal in those violent times to endorse the persecution of
heretics and unbelievers, such as the Bogomils, who were
widespread in the Serbian kingdom. The Catholic church had
declared a crusade against the Albigensian heresy, as they were
called in France and Spain, and Sava's own father had let loose
bloody repressions against them. Sava instead urged persuasion and teaching to win them over. As we look back at him
and his work from the perspective of the persecuted Serbian
church, and particularly during the second World War, St

Sava's legacy shines bright indeed. He powerfully influenced his young church to use peaceful means against its opponents.

Archbishop Sava was well known in his own time and travelled often and widely throughout the Christian East. The reverence he inspired became particularly apparent at his death. As Bishop Nicholai recounts, the Bulgarian king wished to keep the body of Sava in the Bulgarian city of Trnovo, where he had died. A long diplomatic struggled ensued. At last the body was transferred to the monastery church of Mileševo. "The Father had returned to his children," concluded Bishop Nicholai. "His tomb in Mileševo became the source of grace, health, and consolation for Serbian generations to come. Nobody ever believed he was dead."

Bishop Nicholai

Bishop Nicholai Velimirovich, the author of this portrayal of the Serbian patron saint, is undoubtedly one of the most outstanding church leaders after St Sava. He was born into a large Serbian peasant family in 1880, about seven hundred years after St Sava's lifetime. His outstanding ability quickly caught the attention of teachers and churchmen; in his twenties he was studying in Switzerland, England, and Russia. He even reached the United States during World War I, appealing for help for embattled Serbia. In 1918 he was appointed bishop of Žiča, St Sava's see, soon moving to Ohrid until 1934, then returning to Žiča until the collapse of Yugoslavia in World War II. Through his writing as well as his preaching, he became the best known Orthodox church leader in the country. He showed particular concern for the Bogomoljci, a lay movement which stressed preaching and Bible reading, neglected, they felt, by some parish priests. His dynamic leadership brought them into the life of the church and saved them from sectarian influences. His majesty and the awe in which people held him is movingly portrayed in Rebecca West's BLACK LAMB AND GRAY

FALCON, when she describes his handing out red eggs during the Paschal season.

Bishop Nicholai was as well known outside his country, in Orthodox communities abroad as well as in wider Christian circles in the English-speaking world. Edward West, Canon of St John the Divine Cathedral in New York, describes the impact he made when he was invited to Westminster Abbey during World War I: "The Archimandrite Nicholai Velimirovich came, and in three months left an impression that continues to this day. His works, THE LORD'S COMMANDMENTS and his MEDITATIONS ON THE LORD'S PRAYER electrified the Church of England. His vision of the Church as God's family, as over against God's empire, simply shattered the West's notion of what it had regarded as the Caesaro-Papism of Eastern Orthodoxy." ("Recollections of Bishop Nicholai," KALENDAR, Serbian Orthodox Church of USA and Canada, 1979). He also returned to the United States after the war, where he became acquainted with the other Orthodox churches on this continent as well as with the leaders of the Episcopal Church in America.

World War II struck when Bishop Nicholai was at the height of his influence. During the war he shared the suffering of his people. The Independent Croatian State, under German auspices, massacred about 750,000 men, women and children, including Orthodox bishops, large numbers of priests, monks and nuns. Thousands more were sent to death camps in Germany. Under German occupation civil war broke out in Serbia between Tito's Partisans on the one hand and Mihajlovic's Cetniks and the Serbian monarchist Volunteers on the other. In this chaotic situation, Bishop Nicholai, together with Patriarch Gavrilo, was isolated and eventually sent to the Dachau concentration camp.

At the end of the war, Tito executed and imprisoned those who has opposed him as well as any who had reason to resist the revolution he propagated. The church, like all other potentially independent institutions, was silenced and persecuted. Many thousands of citizens, confronted with this new terror, found themselves outside the borders and decided not to return home. Like them, Bishop Nicholai faced the question of whether to return to Yugoslavia with Patriarch Gavrilo or to remain in exile for the rest of his life. He realized that he could not continue to work for his people in the country of his birth, but was now destined to serve them in a foreign land. He knew that in postwar Yugoslavia he would not be given freedom to preach and teach. He chose exile, to serve those who were abandoned, persecuted, weak and poor, who needed their most celebrated spiritual leader, their shepherd.

He arrived in the United States in 1946 as a refugee, without any official position in the church. He found that his presence and his counsel were not well received by the Serbian bishop then in Libertyville, Illinois, and he moved to St Tikhon's Monastery and seminary in Pennsylvania to teach and continue his writings. Despite his health, weakened after the concentration camp, he was in constant touch with the Serbian and other Orthodox communities. His students at St Tikhon's Seminary and Monastery remember him affectionately and respectfully.

In a letter addressed to the graduates of St Tikhon's in 1953, Bishop Nicholai warned them about "the temptation of insignificance." The Orthodox Church nowadays plays an insignificant role in the world, he wrote, where so many millions of Orthodox are oppressed and silenced. But those who are about to be ordained to the priesthood should not be ashamed of the "apostolic suffering" of their church. They should see those hardships in the light of a larger perspective, the history of the Orthodox Church, which is "not only apostolic in doctrine but in suffering too." Because Christians through their sufferings will draw other men to Christ, there is reason for rejoicing and not for yielding to the temptation of despair at the seeming insignificance and powerlessness of their church. As St

Paul wrote: "We are treated... as unknown, and yet well known; as dying, and behold we live; as punished, and yet not killed; as sorrowful, yet always rejoicing; as poor, yet making many rich; as having nothing, and yet possessing everything" (II Cor 6:8).

He was best known to the Orthodox as well as to the wider English-speaking world for his preaching. His sermons were carefully organized and delivered. He used to advise priests not to "make more than three points in a sermon." His sermons were inspired by his vision of Orthodox dogma, permeated by the spirit and achievement of Orthodox spirituality. They were full of power and not simply eloquence.

He was a master of the art of oral communication. Often his written works, like poetry, demand to be read aloud. His sentences, rolling one after another, often with rhymes and puns that made them memorable, conveyed a sense of purpose, power and spontaneity. His sayings, striking in their simplicity, clarity and beauty, are still remembered and repeated many years later by those who heard him.

Many remember one of his first sermons, in New York City on the Sunday of Orthodoxy, 1946. Speaking forcefully regarding the future that faced the Orthodox jurisdications in the new world, he expressed the hope that "a time may not be far off when there will be a United Orthodox Church in America which will include all present eastern national churches in this country." A new arrival, he spoke prophetically as one who understood the movement of time and history and who saw the future. Forty years after this sermon, these words are still a call to overcome our present history, our divisions and separations, with a new history: closer cooperation and unity. He knew well that the Orthodox jurisdictions could not solve their problems properly in isolation, but only by working together.

Bishop Nicholai used to tell of a conversation he had with a spiritual elder on Mount Athos: "Tell me, Father, what is your chief spiritual exercise?" "The perfect visualization of God's presence," answered the monk. Bishop Nicholai went on to say regarding the monk's answer: "Ever since, I tried this visualization of God's presence. And as little as I succeeded, it helped me enormously to prevent me from sinning in freedom and from despairing in prison. If we kept the vision of the invisible God," he concluded. "we would be happier, wiser and stronger in every walk of life."

This vision of God's presence sustained him and gave him strength to work under any conditions that life imposed upon him. Whether he worked in the setting of the monasteries of Žiča and Ohrid as the ruling bishop or in the circumstances of his exile, within the confining walls of a small room, with a bed and a larger desk, he kept up the same steady effort. As students we would visit him and hear his recollections of his life and activities as bishop, how he received visitors, discharged his administrative responsibilities, visited church communities, taught and preached during the day. "But the night was mine," he would say with a certain satisfaction. This was the time for meditation, prayer and writing.

When he came from St Tikhon's to the Serbian church house in New York, we would see the visitors pour in to see him, to greet him or to ask for his spiritual advice and help. He listened to young and old with interest. When physical weakness overcame him, he would withdraw temporarily, then reappear to listen, to comment, to give his blessing.

The Serbian emigration after the war was rent with hostility and distrust. He tried to bring peace among them, treating each spokesman, each individual, fairly and equally, disregarding his political orientation. He maintained his loyalty to the patriarchal church in Belgrade; the Serbian Church in America split into two groups only in 1963, seven years after his death.

He was particularly interested in young emigrants who needed to complete their education, to become priests and laymen in the Orthodox Church. Lacking funds of his own to help them, he turned to his friend Canon West at St John the Divine, who made it possible for several Serbs he nominated to obtain university and theological education. Canon West, who saw Bishop Nicholai in very grand circles as well as in the Serbian church among his people, has written of him affectionately and admiringly: "Whether it be a garden party at Buckingham Palace or dining with the Archbishop of Canterbury, or watching with detached pleasure while a group of his beloved Serbs were dancing a "kolo," or comforting a widowed "popadija," he was always the same beautiful person." He had the gift of "true humility."

He died at St Tikhon's Monastery, and almost immediately his body was removed to the Serbian monastery of St Sava in Libertyville, Illinois, for burial. His name and memory has been revered and kept alive among all the Serbian groups in diaspora, as well as by the faithful in the country of his birth. But he was constantly attacked by representatives of the official Yugoslav press, and this continues to the present. The story of his life, like so much recent history, has been falsified. But now he has defenders in the Serbian church who are protesting these historical distortions and asking for a restoration of his rightful place — for this unusual bishop — in the history of his people. His memory must be restored for the sake of the growth of the church at home and abroad. Those of us who were fortunate enough to know him well during his exile bear witness that he was consistent to his vision and his mission throughout his life, in exile as well as in his homeland.

Within the relatively brief period he had left after the war, Bishop Nicholai published a number of books and articles, as well as leaving some unfinished writings that are still to be collected and published. Living abroad, he felt it was particularly important to help his people understand their faith. He established the Serbian Biblical Institute, for which he wrote in English several small informative tracts, addressed to a general Orthodox audience. Among the books the first is THE HARVEST OF THE LORD, which consists of his meditations upon Christ and his victories, his harvests, and which conveys the underlying message not to despair. Although his church was persecuted and dispersed, he reminds us that Christ was victorious and will always be so.

At the time of his death, he was working on his last book, "Jedini covekoljubac" (The Only Lover of Man), an unfinished manuscript. We may reflect that no book on Christ can ever by really complete, for Christ is still gathering his harvest. When the end comes he will deliver "the Kingdom to God the Father after destroying every rule and every authority and power" (I Cor 15:24). At odd moments he would jot down his thoughts in pencil on small pads, "Misli," which are treasured by those who have seen them but have not yet been collected.

His book on St Sava, published in English in the United States, was written to remind the English-speaking Serbian Orthodox of their spiritual father and to preserve his memory for future generations. He also aimed to bring the Orthodox together by recognizing a great saint that belongs to them all. As the reader will see, it is intended for a general audience: such a text is far more difficult to write than a scholarly one. We see in Bishop Nicholai's presentation that he was a master who had full command of the primary sources and specialized interpretations, had meditated on his theme over many years and was free to present the material in a way that is personal, yet true to the historical picture.

The book also reflects Bishop Nicholai's life and struggles. St Sava heard mysterious voices commanding him to "build something for your people" that can serve as a "harbor of salvation," and he started the renovation of Hilandar. All his life, Bishop Nicholai was involved in building "modest little houses" — as he used to characterize his books to us. His LIFE OF ST. SAVA, "a little house," is an expression of his love for the greatest Serbian "builder," and the sign of his commitment to the saint who christianized the Serbian people. He also writes about St Sava's inclination to deep meditation as well as to action. The author shared these two qualities with his subject and therefore he writes about it with ease and naturalness.

He also reveals something about himself in his meditation on the end of St Sava's life. Disappointed with the struggle within the ruling body of the young Serbian kingdon, Sava withdrew to his House of Silence in Studenica and offered a prayer to God "to let him die in a foreign country." Why did he pray for this? Bishop Nicholai considers several reasons: Sava's protest against political disorder at home, his appeal to the conscience of his people, and his conviction that he would work for their salvation from the outside. These three reasons probably influenced the Bishop's decision to come to America and not to return to Yugoslavia after the war.

Bishop Nicholai had many gifts. What he received he used for the benefit of the Church and his people. Above all, Bishop Nicholai had the rare gift of spiritual leadership. He was a good shepherd of his flock. Starting as a shepherd of his father's sheep, he became the Shepherd of his people, both in war and peace, at home and in diaspora. He shared with his flock its triumphs and tragedies. And his flock remember Bishop Nicholai — the Shepherd, the Preacher and the Teacher, Churchman and Prophet, true successor to St Sava.

Veselin Kesich
Crestwood, New York

CHAPTER 1

THE FATHER

The father of the hero of this story was called Nemanja. He was the first of the Christian Serbian princes to bear this name. Usually they had Slavic names, such as Mutimir, Vlastimir, Chaslav, Voislav, Bodin, Dragomir, Zavida, and Tihomir; these fine old names had a clear meaning to the Slavic-speaking people.

The name Nemanja was appropriate for this strenuous nation builder and unifier. His biblical namesake Nehemiah built the ruined walls of Jerusalem with the permission of the Persian emperor Artaxerxes; his masons "with one hand labored on the work and with the other held his weapon" ready to fight the molesting enemies (Neh 4:17). Nemanja also had to build and to defend his state at the same time until the end of his rule.

According to chroniclers, Nemanja was born in 1113 and died in 1199. His life filled almost a whole century. For nearly half of it he worked and fought for the unity of the Serbian people and for their country. He was born in Ribnica, near old Ducleja, and was baptized first by Latin-speaking priests there, but later rebaptized by clergy recognized by the Patriarch of Constantinople in the Church of the Holy Apostles at Ras. His father was Zavida, one of the provincial Serbian princes, whose capital was Ducleja, the present city of Podgorica in Montenegro. We do not know Zavida's lineage or his family relations with the other Serbian princes. His name has been preserved in history only through the fame of his son Nemanja.

After Zavida's death, Nemanja inherited the easternmost quarter of his princedom, from Ras to Niš, apportioned to him by the will of his father. The other three parts were inherited by his three brothers, Tihomir, Miroslav, and Starzimir. Now

1

there were in existence several Serbian princedoms, the number of which increased by the dismemberment of Zavida's state. Each of these independent small states was in constant danger of becoming a prey of its stronger neighbors. Of the four brothers, the far-seeing Nemanja alone thought of the Serbian people as a whole, and of one Serbian state encompassing all the Serbs.

To achieve his ideal of uniting all the Serbs into one state which could be defended and developed culturally, Nemanja had to struggle long and hard, both against his narrow-minded brothers and relatives and also against almost all his neighbors, big and small. His fortunes shifted back and forth. Once he was defeated by his brothers, and, like Joseph of old, was thrown into a deep pit. Miraculously saved by St George from that pit, he continued the fight. In a successful battle which followed, he forced two of them to surrender and pledge obedience to him by oath, while the eldest, Tihomir, perished. Thus Nemanja became the only ruler of Zavida's state. Miroslav and Strazimir remained loyal to him until the end.

Now Nemanja turned against his external enemies. He fought against Byzantium, Hungary, Dubrovnik, Bulgaria and the Crusaders. In the end he succeeded in creating a Serbian state from the Adriatic to Sofia.

Like many warriors, Nemanja was a very religious man. Whenever he had a pause between battles he built churches, some of them very wonderful ones. The queen of his votive churches, still existing, is Studenica. Others are St George of the Columns (*Djurdjevi Stubovi*) on the Lim River, Archangel Michael in Skoplje, St Panteleimon in Niš, the Holy Virgin and St Nicholas in Kossica. Besides, in a universal Christian spirit, he sent rich donations to the churches of the Holy Virgin the Benefactress in Constantinople, St Dimitrios in Thessalonika, Sts Peter and Paul in Rome, St Nicholas in Bari, St John of Jordan, St Theodosios in Palestine, to the Church of Resurrection in Jerusalem, and others. His generosity toward the poor and destitute was well known in the East and in the West. Nemanja was a mighty warrior for his country and a charitable man of God.

What impression did Nemanja make on his contemporaries? He was a very wise man. When the Byzantine Emperor Manuel (1143-1180) met Nemanja in Niš for the first time, "he was astonished by the wisdom of the young man." Two distinguished chroniclers describe Nemanja as they saw him in Constantinople as a prisoner. Evstathios, who witnessed Nemanja as a captive in Constantinople, wrote: "I have seen Nemanja with admiration; he is in stature greater than nature bestows upon men, very tall and nice looking." And Manas, another chronicler, also describes Nemanja as a powerful man: "a barbarian, broad-shouldered and a fair looking man; he adorned the Emperor's triumph although greeted with derision by the populace of Constantinople."

There are frescoes of Nemanja in many monasteries, in Serbia, Mount Athos and Bulgaria, which accord with the above description. Here he is always portrayed as an old monk of over eighty. Yet even in these pictures he is presented as a man with classical features of grace and strength.

CHAPTER 2

PRINCE RASTKO

The Serbian people are very fond of children and consider many children a great blessing to a family.

Nemanja and his wife Anna had two sons and several daughters. Then they ceased to have children for a long time, yet they desired to have more. Thus they began to pray most fervently to God to gladden them with a third son "who will be a consolation to our souls, the heir of our dominion, and the scepter of our old age." They vowed that if they were given what they asked, they would henceforth live as brother and sister, and never more as a husband and wife. The Lord God in His boundless mercy bestowed upon them a male child. It was indeed a wonderful child, fair looking and bright. At the baptism they gave him the name of Rastislav, Rastko for short.

The more Rastko grew the more he was loved not only by his aging parents and close relatives but by all the courtiers. The happy parents looked at the child with love and with holy awe, as if he were not born of them but was sent from heaven. The courtiers and visitors said of him: "This child is going to be a new sign to the world."

As a boy, Rastko was educated by the best teachers his loving parents could obtain for him. Both in learning and conduct he was a joy to his teachers. When he was fifteen, Nemanja gave him a province to gain experience in ruling and administering, according to tradition present-day Herzegovina. He assigned to the young prince some of the elder statesmen and officers to guide him in princely duties and train him in military arts, as well as some of the sons of noblemen for company in sports and the enjoyment of life.

We know very little about the young prince's life, but the loving memory of the Serbs has passed on to us many pious traditions. We are told that Rastko eagerly and obediently followed the instructions of his elders. While he did not shun some of the pleasures of life with his young companions, he enjoyed them moderately, never to excess. He learned to know the value of recreation and sports. Always kind, bright and animated, he went in company to public games, the theater, hunting, and especially military exercises. He never took part in unrestrained pleasures, such as immoderate indulgence in eating and drinking. It was said of him that he always smiled but never laughed. By his abstinence, he often put to shame his immoderate comrades. He did not rebuke them with cross words or angry looks; his personal life was a sufficient rebuke to them. Instead of spending his free hours in vanity, he read serious scrolls and parchments his father obtained for him, especially those on religion and history. He regularly attended church services, prayed, fasted and gave charity to the poor. He was admired by all because of his purity, and loved because of his incomparable generosity.

CHAPTER 3

A FOILED WEDDING

In those days the custom of early marriage was widespread. The sentimental reason for this was the desire of parents to see grandchildren soon; there was also a moral reason: to save youth from corruption, and a practical one: to get some helping hands for agriculture and handicrafts as soon as possible. The Orthodox Church even in our times permits the marriage of a boy of seventeen.

A special reason for the desire of Nemanja and Anna to see Rastko married in his eighteenth year was their increasing age. Therefore they sent him an invitation to come to the capital after two years' absence.

The capital of the Grand Župan was Ras, a town in a narrow fertile valley encircled by mountains, now called Novi Pazar. It was near the ancient church of the Holy Apostles, in which Nemanja had been baptized.

Far from the royal luxuries of more recent times, the Balkan kings and rulers of Nemanja's day lived a simple life, as was true even in the court of Constantinople, the capital of the empire. According to history and poetry, the Grand Župan Nemanja was a rich ruler. Nevertheless, as a Christian and a warrior, his life was one of simple manners and simple living. His residence was a large rectangular place walled for protection with battlements and watch turrets at every angle. In the center of that square was his house of two stories, over an underground cellar. The cellar served for keeping wine, mead and different foodstuffs. Ice was made of snow in special pools during the winter. The first floor was built of stone. A big fireplace served as a kitchen. The dining room was adorned with a carved wood ceiling and alcoves, containing dishes, plates, gilded wooden spoons, wine cups of wood or ceramic,

6

of oxen horn or beaten gold, and other utensils. Around a low dining table the people sat on three-legged wooden chairs. The upper floor was of wood, plastered inside. Many carved alcoves contained folded mattresses, pillows, woolen blankets. They slept on the carpeted floor. There were also special rooms with colored chests and wardrobes for clothes and still others for arms. Here shields, bows, spears, maces, armor and other arms, hanging on pegs, covered the walls of those rooms. There was also a small house chapel with precious ikons and lamps. At the ikon of St. Stephen the first martyr a lamp was burning day and night, for St. Stephen was the patron saint of Nemanja's family. Special apartments were designed for close relatives and friends.

In the courtyard of the main house, there was a large one-story building for the State Assembly, another for foreign visitors, and a third for officials, secretaries, interpreters, messengers, guards and servants. Outside and around the walls there was another courtyard, also protected by a second wall and battlements. There were buildings for soldiers, falconers, shieldbearers, caretakers of hunting dogs and of horses, and so on. Outside these second walls there were other buildings, huts and tents for lodging and feeding visitors and the poor.

Escorted by noblemen at his service, Prince Rastko arrived at his father's house, in which he was born. He kissed the hands of his parents and they embraced him, the mother weeping for joy, and the father proudly looking at his youngster, whose stature now almost equaled his own.

There he was again, before their eyes, the person closest to their hearts! The beloved son, whom they had long desired to see! With his experienced piercing eyes Nemanja looked at Rastko again and again, and saw before him a tall and slender youth, with reddish hair and blue eyes, amiable, vivacious, erect, quite a grown up knight. Indeed, a wonderful young man matured for marriage, thought he.

The feast started, and lasted for days and weeks. The minor

župans, princes, flagbearers, and motley masses of people crowded the town of Ras and the court of the Grand Župan. All were eager to see and greet Rastko Nemanjic, already the most popular nobleman of Serbia.

As usual the mother was the first to speak to Rastko of his marriage, then the other close relatives, and the father last. Rastko listened politely, either smiling, or giving an evasive answer, careful not to hurt his old parents. Meanwhile, they watched his behavior and found him sometimes absent-minded or deep in meditation. They saw him leave the banqueting company early. They found him at night in the house chapel on his knees praying and sighing deeply.

Among other people then in Ras there was also a group of black-garbed monks from Mount Athos, the Holy Mountain. All of them were Serbs except the leader, a Slav from Kievin Rus. As usual they came to offer prayers and to ask help for their monasteries. The generosity of the Serbian Grand Župan was well known to them. And it was not the first time they came to Ras. Nemanja like them because of their spiritual wisdom and their church services in the Slavonic tongue. Nemanja very much needed Serbian monks for his own monasteries and he might have asked them to take some of the young and willing Serbs with them to the Holy Mountain and train them for service in their native country. He was far from guessing whom they would take with them.

Rastko spent hours and hours talking with those monks. He listened attentively as their leader spoke of the vanity of the worldly life and of the Holy Mountain as the most wonderful refuge from that vanity, the very threshold of the Kingdom of Heaven. Some relatives informed his parents of these talks, and they became apprehensive.

Finally his parents spoke to Rastko more firmly, stressing to him the value of conjugal life for his own personal happiness and also the need of the State. They presented for his choice the names of the best girls, some were Serbian noblemen's daughters and some were foreign princesses. Any imperial or royal court in the Balkans or its neighborhood would be only too glad to give a princess in marriage to the son of the Serbian Grand Župan, who was then powerful and very rich compared to rulers in that part of the world. Except Nemanja himself, all the descendants on the throne were subsequently married to foreign women, for better or for worse, from Vukan to Stefan, Menaja's sons, to Tsar Uroš, the last of the dynasty, the son of Tsar Dusan.

Rastko was very much moved by the reasonable pleadings of his parents, and with unreserved love he kissed their hands, reluctant to consent. But their hearts sensed that his answer would be negative. Their hope revived however when one day he asked his father for permission to go with his friends to the mountains for hunting. His old parents were cheered. They were much pleased that their Rastko would be getting away from those monks, and be in gayer company.

They blessed him and kissed him caressingly without the least idea what that moment meant. It meant not only that their plans were shattered and the wedding foiled but that they would be separated from Rastko for a long time.

CHAPTER 4

THE FUGITIVE

"Vanity of vanities, all is vanity." These words were written twenty-one centuries before Rastko by an aged king who had drunk deep of the cup of pleasures of this world. Nearing death and expecting nothing but dark Sheol after death, this utterance was natural to him.

Seventeen centuries before Rastko, an Indian prince, Gautama Buddha, lived a full and pleasurable life with a wife and a son. In his thirties, he became disappointed with the world, left the royal court, and renounced his family and all bodily pleasures. Retiring to the forest as a mendicant monk, he proclaimed to his countrymen the deceiving vanity of all worldly life and that salvation lay only in non-being, nothingness or Nirvana.

Likewise a contemporary of our Serbian prince, Francis of Assisi, went first through all the turbid waters of an impure life before he awoke and abandoned all the false allurements and fascinations of the world for the sake of Christ.

Unlike these holy men, Rastko had already perceived the vanities of our world by the age of seventeen. Although he had not experienced all worldly pleasures, he understood their painful end. Without committing any grave sin, he knew its sinister consequences. And without giving himself over to any fleshly passions, he observed on others their gnawing and consuming effects.

An ancient writer wrote of Rastko: "He meditated and understood how kingdoms and riches, worldly glory and luxury are tumultuous, changing and disappearing; he also looked and saw all visible beauty and opulence fading away like shadows."

Such a world was disappointing to Rastko. Unusually intelligent and highly emotional, he surveyed the worldly panorama constantly changing, the wheel of human destiny rolling quickly, and the bottomless pit of death swallowing all. Is then death absolute and life accidental in this universe? Christ had revealed and proved that this was not so. Therefore Rastko wanted to betroth his soul to the Lord of Life. It is clear then why he shunned any other betrothal. His young soul was longing for the best, the steadiest and the highest mate. The monks of the Holy Mountain helped only to water the seed which was already deeply rooted in Rastko's heart.

There was only one strong bond which made the young prince waiver for a while—the love of his parents. But even this bond loosened when he heard the old monk stressing Christ's words: "He who loves father or mother more than me is not worthy of me" (Matt. 10:37). Rastko was forced to use a ruse to escape from his parents. However painful it must have been, he made a skillful stratagem to get away. Or was this the plot of the cunning monks? We do not know. The hunting was only a pretense. The monks went on ahead, arranging with Rastko where to meet them. Now the hunting company riding on horseback reached the forest at sunset. Rastko asked his companions to have dinner and then go to the other side of the forest to drive forth the wild animals, while he with a few friends would lie in wait. But after a good dinner the young men fell asleep. Rastko then quickly got into the saddle of his charger and soon reached the prearranged spot where the monks were awaiting him. Now all on horses, they rode with great speed to a strange land far away.

A dark night was covering the sleeping Balkans. With a throbbing heart Prince Rastko, son of Nemanja, a fugitive from all the glitter of this world, hurried into a future shrouded in darkness.

CHAPTER 5

A DESPERATE CHASE

In this world, love is inseparable from pain. The greater the
love the greater the pain at separation.

His hunting companions sought Rastko in vain all of the
following day. Frightened by the absence of their lord, they
reluctantly returned to Ras. Their startling report fell like a
thunderbolt upon the people still feasting at the court, particularly, of course, upon Nemanja and Anna. Their joy turned
into deep sadness and loud lamentation. Some thought the wild
beasts had torn and devoured Rastko.

The Grand Župan, overcoming his own grief, consoled Anna
by saying: "The Lord who gave him to me will help me to see
him again." Then he called his chief of staff and ordered him
to take some officers and start at once in the direction of
Salonika and go, if necessary, even as far as the Holy Mountain to overtake Rastko and bring him back home. He also
handed to the chief a personal letter for the military governor
of Thessalonika. Nemanja requested the governor to find
Rastko and return him, or otherwise he would be threatened
with hostilities.

And now, this group of Serbian noblemen on their chargers
hastened without respite over the mountains and the valleys of
the Balkans in pursuit of Rastko. The governor of
Thessalonika received them with honors. He was troubled by
Nemanja's letter, however. Strongly protective of his friendship with the powerful Serbian ruler, he apprehensively started
the investigations in and around the city. Watchmen were put
on the roads, travelers were screened, caravans were stopped
and the city police alerted, all to no avail. Of course the old
monk was wise enough not to provoke suspicion. He knew all
the secluded paths and trails outside of Thessalonika. The
12

governor wrote a stern letter to the Protos, the head of the
monastic government of the Holy Mountain, urging him to
give up the prince instantly "lest our friend and the father of
the boy become our enemy."

After wearisome travel from Thessalonika along the triden-
tate Chalcidice Peninsula, the Serbian troopers reached the
Holy Mountain, where at once they learned that a group of
Serbs had arrived at the Monastery of St Panteleimon, then
called the Monastery of Thessalonika. They proceeded up the
hill to the small Rassik, where they found Rastko at last. He
was still wearing his secular clothes. They greeted him with due
respect. The chief of staff motioned Rastko aside and had a
long talk with him. He described to him the grief and despair of
his old parents and urged him to obey the order of the Grand
Župan and get ready at once to return home with them.

Rastko, caught unawares, tearfully asked the chief to let him
alone. "You are a man of power, my dear lord," pleaded
Rastko, "and if you only will you can quiet my father and let
me accomplish what I have come here for." The chief not only
did not comply with his wish, however, but threatened to bind
the young man with ropes as a prisoner and take him away.
Unable to persuade the obstinately conscientious chief, Rastko
embraced him and said: "Let God's will be done." He promised to be ready on the following day to go with them. He urged
the chief to have a good rest. But in his mind he hatched a plan,
together with the abbot of Panteleimon. After midnight the abbot ordered a hieromonk to take Rastko to the chapel of the
tower, Pyrgos, in the Rassik Monastery and make him a monk.
The hieromonk did as he was commanded. Rastko took the
prescribed monastic vows, and the hieromonk cut his hair,
clothed him in a monk's black garb, read the prayers and
changed his name. Rastko's new name was Sava. His
celebrated namesake was St Sava the Sanctified of Jerusalem,
who lived in the sixth century.

When the chief of staff awoke in the morning, he sought

Rastko, but could not find him. He became angry with the monks, especially with the old one who had persuaded the young prince to flee away from his father's home to the Holy Mountain. His soldiers in their fury could not refrain from abusing and even beating the monks. Hearing this confusion, the struggles and the cries of the injured brothers, Sava appeared at the small window of the Tower Chapel, called the chief of staff, threw at his feet the bundle containing his nobleman's robes together with his shorn hair, and said: "Take this to my parents and tell them that you have seen me as a monk, with the name Sava." He also gave him a letter for his parents, informing them of what he had done and asking them to forgive and forget him.

Now the chief of staff was completely helpless. According to ecclesiastical law, a monk is secure from the persecution of secular authorities. He is inviolate.

In despair the chief shouted, "O, you merciless boy with a heart of stone! You deceived your father and now us too! How do you not fear God?" Such and even severer reproaches the Serbian officers shouted in anger from below the tower. They shouted and they wept. Sava wept too.

On that memorable morning Prince Rastko was gone forever, and Sava stepped on the stage of the dramatic history of the Holy Mountain, Serbia, and Orthodoxy.

CHAPTER 6

THE DOMINION OF
THE HOLY VIRGIN

Mount Athos, or the Holy Mountain, is a strange country--
the strangest in the Balkans and in the whole Orthodox world.
It is situated 200 kilometers east of Thessalonika and 300
kilometers west of Constantinople. On the map you can see the
Chalcidice Peninsula with three narrow but long promontories
like three arms stretched in the Aegean Sea. The first is called '
Longos, the second Cassandra, and the third (the easternmost)
Athos or the Holy Mountain. While the first two are bare and
waterless, the Holy Mountain is covered with greenery and is
very rich with water. The chestnut and the fir forests give
timber and fuel in abundance. The fertile slopes, glens and little valleys are good for vineyards, orchards and gardens. It is
also rich in olive and fig trees, walnuts and hazelnuts, as well as
in shrubs and bushes with sweet fragrance. To travel on foot or
on mules, still the main means of travel, it would take three to
four hours to cross and three days to travel the length of it.

According to historical legend, Athos had been from time
immemorial a pagan sanctuary. There was at first a shrine of
Apollo, from which came the most ancient name of the whole
land—Apolloniada. Later on a shrine, an oracle of Athos, a
pagan deity who was reputed to forecast the future, was
established there. The land was inhabited by people of different races who had the Greek tongue in common and lived in
nine towns. The names of some historic personages from Asia
and Europe were connected with this land, such as the Persian
kings Darius and Xerxes, Philip and Alexander of Macedonia,
Aristotle the philosopher, and others.

According to a Christian tradition, the Virgin Mary visited
this Mount about 44 A.D. When she arrived at the harbor, the
demon Athos cried to the multitude of the people: "Go quickly

15

down to the sea and meet the Mother of the Great God Jesus!''
And these were his last words, after which he became silent
forever. The people gladly met the Holy Virgin and eagerly
listed to her preaching the glad news of her Son. Then she proclaimed: "Let this land be forever mine, given to me by my Son
and God." On that occasion, some of the pagans were baptized by Lazarus, whom Christ raised from the dead in Bethany
and who afterwards was the Bishop of Cyprus. He accom-
panied the Holy Virgin from Cyprus to Athos. It is from this
legend perhaps that the veneration of the Theotokos as protector of the Holy Mountain is derived.

The number of baptized persons in Athos increased so much
in time that in the reign of Constantine the Great a bishop of
that territory is mentioned. His name was Makarius, with his
residence in Apollonia now called Ierissos. It was visited by St.
Paul (Acts 17:1). The Emperor Theodosius put this diocese
under the higher jurisdiction of Askolios, the Archbishop of
Thessalonika, as a token of gratitude to Askolios who baptized
him. Theodosius' daughter, Placida, paid a visit to Athos. Her
visit excited still greater interest in this mount among the people in the capital and among many others in Asia and Europe
who desired a peaceful life and a refuge from a turbulent world
torn then by heretical struggles.

Since it became known that the Emperors were protectors of
Mount Athos and that the place was exceptionally suitable for
undisturbed ascetic exercises, many flocked to it and one
monastery after another rose beside log huts and caves. Peter
the Athonite, formerly an aristocrat and a warrior, a recluse
there for fifty-three years (681-734), made the place still more
famous by his asceticism and wonder-working. Many came to
emulate his mode of life. Some of them were relatives of the
Emperors, such as St. Athanasius, the founder of the Great
Lavra, the first monastic community, built in the tenth century. Subsequently a central government was established at
Karyes, a synod with the Protos at its head. Thus a monastic

republic of Mount Athos was established, with great monasteries as autonomous units. The presence of women and eating of meat was strictly forbidden in that dominion of the Holy Virgin: chastity, obedience, personal poverty, prayers and brotherly love were the essential requirements. The monastic rule of St. Basil the Great was generally maintained in the greater monasteries of cenobitic life. All other forms of Orthodox ascetic life, such as sketes, *kellia* and hermitages, were also cultivated on Mount Athos and from there spread eventually to all Orthodox countries. On the Holy Mountain, a skete is a monastery built on the grounds of another monastery; a *kellia* is inhabited by no more than twelve monks. So Athos, once a pagan sanctuary, became by God's providence "Agion Oros," the Holy Mountain of Christendom. It was the spiritual heir of the Egyptian desert, the spiritual center of the Fathers of the Desert, after Christian rule in Egypt gave way to Muslim rule.

Naturally Greeks were the first monks to settle in the Holy Mountain. After them came the Georgians, and then the Serbs, Albanians, Bulgars, Rumanians and Russians. Serbian monks on the Holy Mountain are mentioned before the time of Nemanja. In the twelfth century they were well established there and had several smaller monasteries and *kellia*. Even Rassik, where Sava was tonsured, may have been Serbian. There also may have been Russian monks there with the Serbs, for it has always been the custom of the Holy Mountain not to be nationally exclusive but to have as brothers some monks of different nationalities. This custom still holds.

Thus Rastko, a fugitive from Ras, pledged to life-long celibacy, found spiritual shelter in a monastery in this very strange land called the Holy Mountain, the sacred dominion of the Holy Virgin.

CHAPTER 7

THE APPRENTICE

According to the monastic rule, a person has to be a novice for several years before becoming a monk. The novitiate lasts longer on the Holy Mountain than in other monasteries in the world. Rastko, however, was made a monk without any novitiate, due to pressing circumstances. He spent only a few days in Rassik, and rather as a guest than as a novice, before he changed his name from Rastko to Sava; yet as a monk he went through all the hard apprenticeship, considering himself as a youngster, the last among his brothers.

Sava remained a short time in Rassik, a few months at most. Then he was moved to Vatopedi, the oldest of the great monasteries on the Holy Mountain dedicated to the Holy Annunciation. It happened in this way. When the Feast of the Annunciation came, the abbot of Vatopedi invited the abbot of Rassik, asking him to bring Sava along. In Vatopedi Sava made such a favorable impression upon all the brothers that the abbot asked him to stay with them permanently. The young monk left Rassik, with the consent of his abbot. He remained in Vatopedi for twelve full years.

It was of incalculable value for Sava to live in Vatopedi instead of some Slavic monastery. There he learned Greek to perfection. There was a rich library of all the Orthodox Fathers of the Church in the original Greek. There the peak of the refined Byzantine civilization was displayed: the arts of architecture, painting, poetry, vocal music, wood and stone carving, textiles, calligraphy, articles of gold, silver and copper, skillful tailoring, cooking and diverse handiwork, and even good manners. For Vatopedi is one of the most prominent of the Athonite monasteries, built, rebuilt and endowed by all the Emperors until the end of the Paleologos Dynasty.

18

In such a center of spirituality and civilization, Sava had a rare opportunity to model his character after the best patterns he saw and the best books he read. When we think of all this and also of Sava's later acquisition of a large portion of land which belonged to Vatopedi, on which he and his father built the Serbian Monastery Hilandar, we cannot help seeing God's hand in his removal from Rassik to Vatopedi. We firmly believe that this change of place was prompted neither by Sava's own choice nor by the opportunism of his new superior, but by the far-seeing providence of God.

Let us now go back to Ras. On his return there, the chief of staff reported to the Grand Župan what happened with Rastko and gave him the bundle of his robes and his hair. Now for the second time Nemanja and Anna mourned over their beloved son as over one dead. And indeed Prince Rastko was dead, but the monk Sava was alive. The royal court of Ras again turned into a house of lamentation. Finally, Nemanja, supressing his immeasurable grief, wrote a letter to Sava, imploring him to come home at least for a while. He also sent considerable money to his son for his own needs, for the monastery, and for the poor. As one who understood men and as a loving father, he wanted Sava to make friends with these gifts in a strange land. And Sava did so. With the permission of his superior, Sava traveled all over the Holy Mountain many times. Going barefoot and living only on bread and water, he visited Karyes and first paid homage to the Protos, the head of the monastic government. After that he went to the great monasteries: Koutloumousiou, Iviron, Philotheou, Karakalou, the Great Lavra, and others, where the monks by hundreds lived together according to the rule of cenobitic life. From the Lavra he climbed up to the top of Athos, from which he could survey all of the Holy Mountain, and at a distance see on one side Constantinople and on the other Thessalonika. Enraptured by the wonderful beauty of God's creation, he prostrated himself upon the uppermost rock and with tears thanked the Holy

Virgin for having so graciously received him into her dominion.

Descending from the top of the mountain, Sava visited the
cave of St. Peter the Athonite, and down below it other famous
caves, sketes, kellia and hermitages. A skete looks like a small
village with huts and cabins for two or three brothers. They all
have a central church in which they meet once a week, on Sundays, for the Holy Eucharist, which is followed by a brotherly
meal in the communal refectory near the church. The monks in
kellia live independently in modest buildings with a chapel of
their own. Both the sketes and the kellia are under the protection of one of the great monasteries. The monks obtain bread
partly in exchange for their handiwork (wooden crosses, carv-
ings, ikons, prayer ropes, tailoring, writing), partly from their
tiny gardens which they carefully cultivate, and also by gathering edible wild fruits and herbs. Most of their time is spent in
prayer and meditation. The hermits dwell separately and alone,
hidden from men, in wooden huts "or in dens and caves of the
earth" (Heb 11:38), or even in the open under the big trees in
the dense forests, or under overhanging rocks. In most alarm-
ing places they live on the almost perpendicular slopes of
Athos, known as Karoulia and Kapsokalyvia. They are constantly occupied with prayer and meditation. Their needs are
few and their worries none.

Sava visited all of them, learning their ways of living a holy
life. He gave them gifts and insatiably listened to their
teachings from their experiences. And their experiences,
gathered under such strange circumstances, deeply affected
Sava, as a revelation of a world quite different from the outside
world he had known and lived in up to that particular time.

While on these errands, Sava was twice captured by robbers
and pirates, but both times he had succeeded in getting rid of
them, even bringing them to repentance.

With a world of new experiences, Sava returned to Vatopedi,
serene in temper, rich in knowledge, and eager to serve his God
and his neighbors.

CHAPTER 8

THE BUILDER

A new bag of gold was brought from Ras to Vatopedi, with gold, several chests with altar vessels of beaten gold and silver, made by the renowned goldsmiths of Ras, Prizren and Skoplje, as well as veils and tablecloths of silk and brocade for use in the church and a great quantity of woven materials for the garments of the monks. Horses came too, useful for hauling and riding in a roadless country. Loving parents had sent all these gifts for their beloved son, although they knew well that he would keep nothing for himself.

Sava made good use of these royal gifts. First of all, he distributed alms to the hermits and the kellia. Then he gave to the church what was sent for the church, and to the abbot and the brothers that which was designated for them. He reserved a good deal of the money for the buildings he planned to construct in Vatopedi. The abbot of Vatopedi may have known why he had invited the son of the rich Grand Župan to come and settle in his monastery. Yet, regardless of the petty schemes of men, the Lord keeps in view His great, fixed purpose for His elect.

More new residences were badly needed for the increasing number of monks. Sava built several such residences of two and three stories. One he reserved for himself and his father. Said he, "If God wills it, I and my lord, my father, shall dwell in our own house here." Of course, he did not mean that he and his father alone would occupy the whole house, Konak. He meant that the house would be a Serbian home for Serbian monks in the future.

Thereupon, he started to build three churches, called "parecclesia," like three jewels. The first one, behind the Great Church, he dedicated to the Holy Virgin, the second to St.

21

John Chrysostom, and the third to the Transfiguration of the Lord. This last one was built on top of the highest of ten towers. All three were built of stone and brick and roofed with stone sheets, which were in abundance in the Holy Mountain. He also added a new roof of lead to the Great Church. Besides, he repaired and renovated several other edifices. "And many other things he accomplished in the monastery, too difficult to enumerate." Therefore, the governing board of the monastery honored Sava deservedly with the title of "The second founder of Vatopedi"—the Emperor Theodosius the Great (346-395 A.D.) being counted as its first founder.

It seems that Sava had inherited from his father an inclination to build, to construct. He himself helped in all these constructions, not only as a designer and overseer, but also as a manual laborer. Besides all this work he discharged his daily duties in the church and kitchen. He rowed loaded boats, fished, baked bread, worked in the fields and vineyards, gathered olives and figs, cut wood, traveled as a messenger to the Protos or other monasteries, read at the services and sang in the choir. He was always on hand to help everyone, always ready to serve and obey, always smiling, never tiring, never complaining. His blue eyes radiated sincerity and friendliness. Just as he was the most beloved prince at the court of his father, even so he was the most beloved monk in Vatopedi.

Along with all these external and diverse activities, Sava ceaselessly performed an inward activity, well known in the Orthodox monasteries. While building visible churches of stone, he at the same time, was constantly building the invisible temple of his soul. Looking at created things, he thought of the Creator of all things. Looking at his brother monks, he thought of the angels. His lips were constantly in motion—a habit of all true monks. The reason for this was the repetition of the "mental prayer" which he had learned from the great hermits. The prayer is short: "O Lord Jesus Christ, have mercy upon me"—but the value of this mental prayer is enormous according to the testimonies of those who practice it. It was known by the Fathers in Egypt and on Mount Sinai before the Holy Mountain. The monk practicing it is restrained from vain thoughts, his heart is kept warm, evil spirits are driven away and despair and fear are dissipated. It is attested that those perfected through this inward activity are able to continue to pray even during their sleep. And Sava tried hard to reach spiritual perfection.

All these efforts, the inward and outward, Sava continued relentlessly for ten years in Vatopedi before he again met his aged father. The task had been hard, almost equal to crucifixion, for a young man like him. But with God's grace he endured heroically and succeeded in subduing all evil impulses in body and imagination and supplanting them with holy, pure and positive impulses. At the end, his body had no more power over his soul than a chariot has over the charioteer.

During those ten years, Sava and Nemanja exchanged many letters, each one urging the other to come to see him. The father wanted to see his son once more before his death. Sava on the other hand asked his father to come to the Holy Mountain to spend his last days in preparation for the other world. Sava's last letter to Nemanja was very severe and almost threatening. "If you despise my words (invitation)," wrote Sava, "abandon the hope of seeing me in the next life." At the same time he recommended that his mother Anna also take monastic vows in a convent of her own accord.

This letter produced the desired effect. It paved the road for a meeting of father and the son, although not in the homeland of the Grand Župan but in a foreign land, which Sava made a spiritual home for both of them as well as for generations of Serbs to come.

CHAPTER 9

THE FATHER OBEDIENT
TO THE SON

At last Sava prevailed and Nemanja obeyed. In March 1196, the Grand Župan convoked the State Assembly at Ras and announced his abdication. The old man addressed the Assembly more as a father than as a ruler, addressing them as: "My dear children." He then described the deplorable situation of the Serbian people and the Serbian state when he, by God's providence, became their head about forty years before. He told how they had been torn asunder by internal strifes, confused by heretical agitations, imperiled constantly by stronger neighbors, and reduced to poverty and impotence. He went on to tell how he, with God's help and the people's support, had succeeded in defeating all his enemies, enlarged the Serbian State "in length and width" and brought about the unity of the Serbian people. Finally, he exhorted them all to fear God, to keep the Orthodox faith and the law and order he had established, to be loyal to the new Grand Župan, his successor, and to respect the servants of the Church: the bishops, priests, and monks. He finished his address with the words: "Hold firmly to justice and brotherly love among yourselves and forget not charity. Peace be with you all."

Thereafter, he presented to the Assembly his younger son Stefan, saying: "Have this one instead of me. He is a noble branch of my body. I put him on the throne which Christ bestowed upon me."

To his eldest son Vukan he allotted the seacoast province of South Dalmatia, to rule with the title of a prince. Then to both sons he extended a fine exhortation: "My sons," said he, "put your hope in God and do not boast of your wisdom and power. Be not desperate when God castigates you, nor downhearted when he reproves you; for God castigages him whom he loves to make him more perfect. I give you this commandment which is from above: 'Brood no evil against each other, but have true love among you. For he who loves not his brother, loves not God. God is love'."

Then amidst the great cries and lamentations of the people, saddened by the separation from their strong ruler and father, Nemanja proceeded to the church of Sts Peter and Paul with his sons, state dignitaries, and chiefs of staff. Bishop Kalinik of Ras met him at the door of the church. At the end of the prayer, both the bishop and the old Grand Župan put their hands on the head of the kneeling Stefan and blessed him as the new Grand Župan of Serbia. "And now," said Nemanja, "come and let me have with you my last meal as a layman." At the banquet, Nemanja conversed cordially with all those present as a father with his children. And when the banquet was over, he distributed gifts and presents to each one at the table according to his rank and merit, and liberal charities to the poor.

Early on the following morning, Bishop Kalinik received in the same church the monastic vows of both Nemanja and Anna, clothed them in black robes and changed their names—calling Nemanja "Simeon" and Anna "Anastasia." This happened on the day of Annunciation, March 25, 1196. Soon after this ceremony, Simeon and Anastasia separated. Simeon went to his monastery Studentica, and Anastasia to her convent of the Holy Virgin near Kuršumlija. Thus a new life began for both of them.

In Studentica, Simeon lived as a simple monk for about eighteen months, following strictly all the prescribed rules for prayer, fasting, learning and work. He had laid down a weighty load, but had assumed a new one. During this time he established economic order in the monastery, increased the number of monks, fixed his grave in the Great Church and appointed a hieromonk, the worthy Dionysius, abbot over all. Then he took final leave of his country and his people and turn-

ed to the Holy Mountain on October 7, 1197. He was escorted
by the Grand Župan Stefan and other Serbian dignitaries
down to the Greek frontier. Again a very touching separation
took place from Stefan and those who remained behind. With
a few of his most faithful friends, the old man proceeded
through Greek territory and arrived in Vatopedi on November
2, 1197.

The Abbot of Vatopedi, with the brotherhood, received him
with honor and joy. They at once proceeded to the church, the
bells pealing, to sing the Thanksgiving. Then the father and the
son met. Overwhelmed by indescribable emotion, they embraced each other at last, after ten years of separation and yearning! They had separated long ago as Grand Župan Nemanja
and Prince Rastko, and now they met as monk Simeon and
monk Sava in a strange country. Simeon was 84 years old and
Sava 27, like snowy winter and blossoming spring, yet two
hearts equally afire with love of God. Parents and children can
only know how much they love each other after a long separation. They discover, when they meet again, how immeasurable
is that love.

The Protos, on hearing of the arrival of the Grand Župan,
came from Karyes to greet the distinguished newcomer. Simeon in his humility prostrated before him and the Protos
knelt before Simeon, the two greeting and embracing each
other. This was a great event in the history of the Holy Mountain for previously no other great ruler of any Orthodox nation
had come to that dominion of the Holy Virgin to live as a monk
among the poor monks. Also the abbots of all the monasteries
with a multitude of the black-robed monks came to see and
greet the former formidable knight-warrior, now a humble
monk like themselves. Simeon, eager to learn, asked them of
their way of life leading to salvation. He let none leave without
a gift brought from Serbia. For he had brought with him horses
and mules, heavily laden with different gifts, precious ones for
the churches and useful ones for the brothers. The lion's share,

of course, he presented to Vatopedi with two large buckets full of silver and gold.

Then Sava took his tired father to the house he had built especially for the two of them to live in, inseparable until the end of their lives.

CHAPTER 10

HILANDAR

As soon as Simeon had rested, he wanted to go see all of the Holy Mountain. But the rule of all monasteries is that one can go nowhere without the permission and blessing of the superior. Thus, the old man, who once commanded armies, now had to obey a simple monk, the abbot. The permission granted, he started with Sava and some other companions. Sava, however, wanted to go barefoot as usual. Seeing him, his father said, "Spare me, my child, for you strike my heart with those sharp stones upon which you walk with bare feet." Sava obeyed, put on shoes and mounted a horse. Several mules loaded with gifts followed them.

They were received with honor and good will by the Protos in Karyes as well as in all the monasteries and kellia. They gave gifts and presents generously in all these places, so much so that their names were inscribed among the Emperors and Kings as founders. Their fame spread, and even the desert fathers flocked to them from the trackless wilderness. Simeon was especially beneficent to them.

On their return home, Simeon felt very exhausted. And he complained to his son with sighs and tears that he was unable to stand upright, or kneel and prostrate himself in prayer, or fast according to the rule, because of his age and exhaustion. So Sava consoled him by saying: "Do not be sad, my lord and father. I will do your fasting, standing and prostrating before the Lord. Because you have obeyed and followed me, let the Lord seek your soul from me." Such was the great and still increasing love between them.

Now their restless impulse for building appeared again. In addition to the three churches which Sava alone had built earlier, they now built three more. They also constructed more new hospices for the brothers and the pilgrims. They restored the Monastery Prosphora, which had been destroyed by pirates. And they planted new vineyards and orchards. It is no wonder their full portraits were later painted at the entrance of the Great Church, as the new founders of Vatopedi.

Meanwhile, Sava found the ancient ruins of a monastery called Hilandar which belonged to Vatopedi. He spoke to the abbot about its restoration, although that depended on the Emperor of Byzantium. Therefore, Sava, with the abbot's permission, went to Constantinople and obtained a sealed document from the Emperor, by which Vatopedi was permitted to restore Hilandar as its dependency.

But then something unexpected happened. A mysterious man paid a visit to Sava and said: "You love strangers and the poor. You have done very much for the foreign monasteries on the Holy Mountain, particularly for Vatopedi. Take now my advice as from one who speaks to you in the name of God. Find a place and build a monastery for your own people and call it the Serbian Monastery. It will be a harbor of salvation for many of your own nation."

Hearing this, Sava hurried to inform his father of the sudden message. And Simeon "awoke as from sleep" and greatly rejoicing said: "I presume it was an angel sent by God." They first presented to the abbot their wish concerning Hilandar. The abbot refused them bluntly. They spoke to the Protos and he gladly approved their plan.

Simeon wanted to see the place himself. Too weak to ride on horseback, he was put in a palanquin between two horses. Thus, he saw the place, the ruins, the forests, the olive trees and the sea harbor of Hilandar, and was very much pleased. He left his country and his people to forget and to be forgotten, to be dead to this world and alive only to the next one. But now his eyes were opened and he clearly understood that God had brought him and his son to the Holy Mountain, not merely for their personal salvation, but to use them also as instruments for an unusual service to their own Serbian people. Now his own patriotism flared up again in his heart.

The monks of Vatopedi, however, resisted for a long time. They calculated well the losses to their own monastery if they let the Serbs go. But under the constant insistence of Simeon and the pressure of the Protos, they gave in. The abbot said to his community: "We have received many rich gifts from them; let them not go away angry with us. If we give them Hilandar, they will be our friends forever."

Now as soon as the legal document was signed by the abbot of Vatopedi and the Protos, Sava received the blessing of his former abbot and at once started work in Hilandar. He hired a great number of workers and artists from near and far. In a relatively short time he built the church, residences and cells for the brothers, for gold and silver were flowing in abundance from the Grand Župan Stefan. When Stefan was informed of what his father and brother had in mind, he was very much pleased. When all the main work had been finished, Sava transferred his father to Hilandar.

A number of the Serbian monks who until then lived in deserts or in foreign monasteries gladly joined the brotherhood of the Serbian monastery. Noblemen and servants who had come with Simeon from Serbia took monastic vows. So the brotherhood quickly grew. Sava, in accord with Simeon, appointed an abbot in the person of a hieromonk, the worthy Methodius. So for the first time in the long history of the Holy Mountain the Serbian people had a great monastery of their own among other great monasteries of Orthodox nations and tongues.

Sava indefatigably proceeded now to acquire much land with abandoned sanctuaries in order to make Hilandar self-sustaining. He received from the Protos many deserted kellia with olive groves and vineyards around Hilandar, and he bought several smaller monasteries with spacious land in Mileia and Karyes.

Simeon was more than pleased with all that Sava had accomplished in such a short time. He was thankful now to be able to live peacefully in expectation of death, not in a foreign land, but in his own Serbian house. Yet he thought of the future of Hilandar as a Serbian sanctuary and property. Though the deed, signed by Vatopedi and by the Protos was a sufficient legal document, he thought something more was necessary. A great secular authority should confirm this transfer and moreover give the privilege of being a wholly independent Serbian monastery to Hilandar.

With this idea in mind, Simeon sent Sava to Constantinople to his friend, the Emperor Alexios Angelos.

CHAPTER 11

A SUCCESSFUL MISSION

The capital of the Byzantine Roman Empire on the Bosphorus glittered with fabulous beauty. Even today neither Naples nor Alexandria nor Bombay can be compared in beauty with Constantinople. But here, as elsewhere, there was a sad disharmony between the external brilliance of a perfect civilization and the inadequacy of men's characters. It is a humiliating fact that man has always been abler and readier to perfect material things rather than himself. This disproportion can be seen in every high civilization. The more precious a civilization, the more debased are its human inhabitants. After the death of Manuel Comnenos in 1180, the empire went into a decline and for a long time it lacked inspired leadership.

In the imperial capital, both Simeon and Sava were treated with respect. In the royal court they were honored as the relatives of the emperor, for Eudokia, the daughter of the then ruling Emperor Alexios Angelos, was the wife of Grand Župan Stefan, Sava's brother. Sava's visit, now the second one, excited great interest in the city.

Emperor Alexios was a good-natured man. He received Sava "with great affection." And Sava charmed him and all others by his perfect manners as a prince and his striking simplicity as a man of God. The first question he put to Sava after a cordial welcome was: "Is the holy old man, your father and my friend, still alive?" Sighing deeply, the emperor said, "He is a man blessed by God, for having won an earthly kingdom, he is now toiling wholeheartedly to win a heavenly one, too."

Alexios, who above all liked good times with his friends, sincerely admired Simeon and Sava. He sighed because he felt incapable of imitating them.

Then Sava handed to the Emperor Simeon's letter, which

made a great impression on him as coming from a holy man. Simeon and Sava asked him to confirm the transaction with Vatopedi removing the Hilandar monastery from its jurisdiction, together with the kellia and other property that Sava had acquired on the Holy Mountain; secondly, to declare and confirm the restored Hilandar to be forever an independent Serbian monastery in such a way that neither the Protos nor anyone else should have any authority over it; and thirdly, to give his own imperial staff, or baton, to be preserved in Hilandar as representing the emperor himself. When the brotherhood elected a new abbot, they were to give him that staff, and he was to receive it from them as from the hands of the emperor himself, receiving with it full and uncontested authority.

The Emperor Alexios readily did all Sava asked of him. He prepared a writ on parchment with his golden seal and signature and with it he handed Sava an imperial staff, representing his own person and his imperial authority. The writ and the staff are preserved in Hilandar until this day.

During his stay in Constantinople, Sava dwelt in the Monastery of the Holy Virgin in Evergetis, the Benefactress. He and his father were considered new founders of that monastery. They restored it from ruins and maintained it by their endowments. Therefore, the Serbian monks felt at home in that monastery. There Sava had the opportunity to continue to live according to his habitual monastic rule. From there he went to see the Great Church of Saint Sophia, Blachernae, and other celebrated churches and shrines of Christian martyrs in Constantinople. He often went also to the royal palace to have conversations with the Emperor. The Emperor and the Empress asked Sava about their son-in-law, Stefan, and their daughter, Evdokia, as he was better informed by the Serbian messengers who came more frequently to the Holy Mountain than to Constantinople. They, of course, asked Sava about spiritual life and religious matters. And they both were strengthened and gladdened by Sava's words. At their last meeting, Alexios said to Sava, "I have fulfilled all your petitions, holy father, and now I beg to ask you to remember us in your prayers to the Lord." Saying this, the Emperor handed to his guest a bag of gold for his father, Simeon. After that, Sava took leave of Alexios and went also to take leave of His Holiness the Ecumenical Patriarch.

Back in the Evergetis, a strange thing happened to Sava. When he was giving alms to the poor, an unknown woman appeared to him and said: "O holy lover of God, the Mother of God the Benefactress ordered me to reveal to you a thing which you need for your work. In the Holy Mountain, near your monastery, in such and such place there are two vessels with gold hidden under the earth. Seek and you will find, and then use it for God's glory." After the mysterious woman vanished, Sava stood musing for a long time in amazement.

Having returned safely to the Holy Mountain, Sava kissed his loving father's hands and reported everything to him. He showed him the Emperor's staff and parchment, with the seal, confirming about Hilandar all they had requested. Simeon was very much pleased. And they wrote at once to Stefan informing him of what they had done, and placing Hilandar under his protection.

After that the old man, weak and exhausted, stretched his body out on a straw mat, with a stone as a pillow. He felt his end nearing.

CHAPTER 12

DEATH OF SIMEON

According to an ancient custom in the Eastern Church, when a person is dying, the relatives, friends and neighbors come to him to ask for his forgiveness.

They say: "Forgive me, dear friend."

The dying person answers: "I forgive thee, and may God forgive thee. Forgive thou me."

"Bless me, and be blessed by God."

"God bless thee, and I bless thee."

"Pray for me."

Such a scene occurred at the death bed of Simeon, too. On February 6th, ill with fever and lying on his coarse, ascetic bed on the floor, he asked for Holy Communion . He communicated every morning for seven days, living only on that without taking any other food.

Sava most devotedly nursed his father day and night. Finally Simeon said: "My most beloved child, the light of my eyes, the comfort and protection of my old age, behold the hour of our separation has arrived." Then he gave the last orders to Sava concerning the monastery and his body. He wanted him to take his dead body in due time to Serbia and bury it in Studenica, in the tomb he himself had prepared years before. He also asked Sava to pray for his soul. "I know, my son, that whatever you ask from God, it will be given to you. And now my soul is in fearful need of your prayers." All in tears, Sava too begged his father to pray in the next world "for all of us, your children in the Lord, for your kinsmen, country and for the churches you have founded." Lastly, he fell on his knees and asked for forgiveness and blessing. His father put his hands upon the son's head and said: "O, my blessing, I bless you!"

After this, all the brothers gathered around their dying

benefactor to receive forgiveness and blessings. When the morning song in the church was almost ended, the holy man himself burst into singing: "Praise ye the Lord, let every breathing creature praise the Lord." With these words he gave up his ghost.

Sava fell on the face of his father "and washed it with warm tears instead of warm water" and kissed his hands many times, then folded them crosswise.

The news of Simeon's death spread quickly over the Holy Mountain, and a great number of monks gathered at Hilandar from all directions. The funeral service was headed by the Protos, and the monks of different nationalities sang, with lit candles in their hands. After the funeral service was performed, the body was buried in the Great Church of Hilandar.

Thus died the former Grand Župan of Serbia, Stefan Nemanja, and of late the simple monk, Simeon, on February 13, 1199. He died in a strange land, yet in his own Serbian monastery.

Simeon and Sava have presented to the world the finest pattern of filial and paternal love. The natural son became the spiritual father of his earthly father. According to the biblical saying: "Instead of your fathers shall be your sons" (Ps 45:16). In the family life of the Serbian people, this pattern of mutual love of parents and children has been highly praised. It has never failed to crown with peace and success those who followed it. God grant that this sublime pattern be followed in the family life of Serbs in our own time and in the future!

Let us now follow Sava's course and destiny. One day he was standing in an olive grove in deep meditation. Suddenly there flashed in his memory the picture of that mysterious woman in Constantinople, who told him of a hidden treasure in the vicinity of Hilandar. It was a time when he was in dire need of money for his work and his charity. He quickly took one of his disciples and went to the spot and they began to dig with spades. Scarcely had they started to dig when the spades struck two metal vessels full of gold. Offering with wonder his thanks to God, Sava took the treasure and divided it into four parts. One part he sent to the Evergetis in Constantinople, the other was kept for Hilandar, and the rest he gave to the poorer monasteries on the Holy Mountain and to needy hermits and kellia. All this he did in memory of his deceased father.

The news of Simeon's death filled the Grand Župan Stefan and all the Serbs with grief and sorrow. On that occasion, Stefan sent to Sava a large sum of money to be used in memory of their father. Indeed, Sava made the best use of this money. He saved three famous monasteries on the Holy Mountain: Karakalou, Xeropotamou, and Philotheou.

Karakalou was in great debt to the Great Lavra. Unable to pay, and in danger of losing its rank and independence, the brotherhood of Karakalou asked the monks of the Lavra to have mercy upon them. They, however, took Karakalou into their possession, driving the abbot and the brothers out. Now helpless in their misery, the monks of Karakalou turned to Sava for help. Hearing their complaint, and deeply hurt by such an injustice of Christians toward Christians, Sava at once paid all their debts to the Lavra, and thus secured their lives and independence.

Xeropotamou, being very much exposed to robbery from the sea port Daphne, had often been plundered and finally ruined by pirates and robbers.

Asked for help, Sava restored that beautiful monastery with the buildings around it, bought back its properties, which had been under mortgage, and paid for the frescoed painting of the whole church. The church is dedicated to the Forty Martyrs (March 9th).

A good Christian man by the name of Philotheos started to build a new and great monastery on the Holy Mountain. But his ambition being grand and his means small, he had to stop the work halfway. There was nobody to help him. So he too went to Sava. Sava came to his place to see his work, improved the plans, and gave a sufficient sum of money to that good man so that the monastery was quickly finished, and God has been praised in it ever since. That monastery still exists, and is called Philotheou.

All these three monasteries have flourished until our day, thanks to Sava's generosity. And all three have recognized Sava as their new founder.

Sava, however, did all these good works not for his own glory but for Christ's love, and in memory of his father, Simeon.

CHAPTER 13

THE HOUSE OF SILENCE

We are going to recount now how Sava instituted a unique
home for spiritual exercises and worship in Karyes, the center
of the Holy Mountain. It is called in Greek "hesychastirion"
—which means "House of Silence". The Serbs call it
"Postnica."

The death of his saintly father may have accelerated Sava's
retirement from the world into solitude. The constant longing
for a solitary, eremitic life never left him. Indeed, that very
longing had drawn him to the Holy Mountain. It increased in
him after he met the real hermits secluded in the huts, caves
and precipices of Athos, unharassed by the world, undisturbed
in meditations, careless of their bodily lives, free as the birds,
having only God for a companion. Their mode of life strongly
gripped Sava's imagination. That is the way to holiness, he
thought. After he first visited them in the early months of his
stay in Vatopedi, he asked the abbot to let him go and live with
those hermits. He was then only seventeen. This was not a
novel request; many young enthusiasts wish to embrace this
way of life. They wish at once to go into isolation and solitude.
They imagine that intercourse with men in a monastery is a hindrance to their direct relationship with God, because they are
ignorant of the struggle the hermits have with a much greater
hindrance: evil spirits. The abbot then strongly opposed Sava's
wish to go away from the monastery. He explained to Sava
how dangerous it was for a monk in his teens to wrestle alone
"against the rulers of the darkness." It might lead to disap-
pointment and frustration or even to insanity, as sometimes did
happen.

But now Sava was a mature man of thirty and had to ask no
superior for permission. He built a small house in Karyes with

a pretty little chapel in it, dedicated to his namesake St Sava
the Sanctified (+ 532). There, in a narrow, dark cell he gave
himself to the most rigorous austerities he had seen or heard of.
With these austerities, as with lashes, he whipped his body and
his soul without mercy. Day and night, in the complete
darkness of his cell, he spent his time in deep meditation on
every sentence in the Gospels, taking time off only for prostra-
tions, weeping and ceaseless prayers. He lay on the bare
ground, fasting to the verge of starvation, mortifying every
fleshly desire, curbing every deviation of his thoughts from
God, urging his heart to cleave inseparably to Jesus Christ
through mental prayer. God alone knows what other exercises
he practiced to purify his soul and make it, as it were, a spire
piercing the heavens.

Crucified without a cross, he emaciated his body so much
"that his belly contacted his spine." Thereby he contracted a
disease of the spleen which he was never able to cure and which
forced him to abstain from any fat or sweet food. He,
however, thanked God for this illness which helped him toward
every moderation. But he gained what he wanted most: il-
lumination of the heart from above and peace of soul beyond
understanding. He also had some marvelous visions of the
heavenly world, in one of which he saw his father in light and
glory. Simeon told him: "You shall be honored with two
crowns, one ascetic and the other apostolic, and both of us
shall enjoy immortal bliss." This apparition Sava understood
as a hint to go to Hilandar for the annual commemoration service at the tomb of his blessed father.

Whatever Sava did or experienced as good and useful, he
wanted to perpetuate for the salvation of others. As he
emulated the perfect spiritual leaders, even so he wanted to be
emulated by his disciples. Therefore he made his House of
Silence a permanent institution connected with Hilandar and
yet independent. He wrote a Rule for that place to be followed
by those in Hilandar who were willing to live in it. This Rule

Sava wrote with his own hand on a parchment, and signed it "the least of all sinners, Sava." It is still preserved, and it is called "the Karyes Typicon." Because it was short, he engraved it on a marble plaque, and put it over the entrance of Postnica, where it still stands. The main prescriptions of this Rule are:

Two or three brothers of Hilandar should live there always.

It ought to be wholly independent from the Protos and even from the Abbot of Hilandar.

The brothers living in Postnica should keep prayers and fasts as prescribed particularly for them, to wit: they are permitted to eat only once a day except on Saturday and Sunday, and must do without olive oil on Wednesday and Friday.

They are obliged to read the whole Psalter every night, and all the Canons to Christ and the saint of the day, as well as the Akathists in praise of the Holy Virgin.

The great Monastery of Hilandar ought to supply the brothers there with the necessary food and clothing.

Now it is over 700 years that this Rule has been strictly observed in the Serbian House of Silence: the fasts are never broken, prayers never cease, and the lights of the lamps are never extinguished. It is a unique prayer house not only on the Holy Mountain, but in the whole Orthodox world. The monks of the Holy Mountain venerate that place and have awe and respect for the brothers living in it.

As it is seen, this Rule is very rigorous, but moderate in comparison with the extreme rigorism of St. Sava. He condescended to the frailty of human nature.

The master builder of visible churches, Sava proved to be the unrivaled master builder of human souls, the invisible temples of the Holy Spirit.

CHAPTER 14

A SAINT REVEALED BY GOD

It is an established fact that in the Eastern Church no person can be considered a saint unless God reveals him to be so. There is no doubt that Sava saw in a vision his dead father Simeon alive and in great glory. Filled with both awe and joy by that vision, he left Postnica and hurried to Hilandar to prepare the annual memorial service to his father.

Purposely he invited the Protos, all the abbots of the great monasteries, the spiritual fathers and anchorites of the Holy Mountain. Meanwhile, he decorated the tomb of Simeon and made other preparations. The invited and the uninvited came in great number. The Protos with many priests performed the usual evening commemorative service, introductory to a great morning liturgy. After the evening meal in Hilandar's large refectory all wanted to go to rest. Sava begged the Protos to maintain the vigil in the closed church during the night with the Greek and the other monks, omitting the Serbians. "And I am going, Father," he said, "to the Pyrgos with my own monks to do the same in our native tongue. And when you see a sign of my late father, send for me." The Protos did not understand the meaning of Sava's words, yet he obeyed and entered the church with the Greek, Georgian and Rumanian priests and monks. Now, Sava gave the key of the church to the Protos. He gave other keys to the key bearer and sent him to rest. He himself, however, went to his cell and prayed all the night through. He asked of God to reveal the glory of his father in public which, thus far, he had revealed only to him in secret in the House of Silence. He wished that the sainthood of Simeon should appear before the eyes of other people, to strangers. "For how will it help me, O Lord, if I alone rejoice in Thy grace toward my father? Show it, pray, to all publicly." So

prayed Sava while the Vigil went on in the closed Great
Church.

At dawn when the clergy solemnly sang "Glory to God on
high," behold, fragrant oil began to flow from the body of Simeon, with a sweet aroma filling the whole church. The monks
in consternation cried, "Kyrie eleison! Lord have mercy upon
us!" Seeing this wonder, the Protos remembered Sava's words:
"When you see a sign, send for me." Quickly he sent for Sava,
who, arriving fell on the tomb and loudly wept and glorified
the Lord.

We presume the readers will now understand Sava's in-
genious stratagem. Believing firmly that the Lord would listen
to his prayers and reveal the holy glory of his father, he did not
want only the Serbs to witness it and proclaim it first. God's
miracle was less bewildering to the Protos than was Sava's
prediction and also the freedom with which he boldly and in-
sistently asked God to do what he wanted. "The Lord does the
will of those who love Him," said the Protos. After the initial
amazement, however, he with all the monks rejoiced exceedingly because God, in His measureless grace, had made
one of them, a poor monk, a great saint, through whom one
more adornment was bestowed upon the Holy Mountain, and
there was one more intercessor for them in Heaven.

Sava filled a flask with oil from St. Simeon's body in order
to send it to his brother, the Grand Župan Stefan. Thus the
supposedly mournful commemorative service turned out to be
a cheerful thanksgiving to God for revealing a new saint to the
Holy Mountain and the Orthodox world at large.

The good Protos Dometius held Sava in his heart with ador-
ing reverence. He often urged Sava to be ordained a priest. But
Sava always declined, saying that he was unworthy of such a
great honor. The Protos said "O, would God I were so unworthy!" Finally, Sava yielded, and Father Dometius rejoiced.
Thereupon the Protos invited Bishop Nicholas of Ierissos to
come and ordain the monk Sava. The bishop came to Hilandar

and at a solemn liturgy ordained Sava first a deacon and on the following day as a priest. On the Holy Mountain it is considered a great honor for a monk to become a priest. Sava received priesthood after he had reached thirty years of age, as required by ancient canons of the Church. The Protos Dometius was so filled with joy that he kissed the hand of the new priest, although he was much older than Sava.

Then Sava went to Thessalonika on a mission for Hilandar. This city has gone through great calamities since, but it was, in Sava's day, still the metropolis of Illyria. It was a wonderful city, protected by great walls with its soaring Seven Towers, Septapyrgon, and with an excellent harbor. Full of Christian memories since the time of St Paul, Thessalonika competed with Constantinople in manifold expressions of Byzantine civilization, in art, architecture, mural decorations, in public and private edifices, in glorious churches painted in fresco, and in venerated tombs and relics of many martyrs headed by the most celebrated of them, St. Demetrios the Patron Saint of the city.

There was a monastery, Philocalos, with Serbian monks in Thessalonika even before Sava's time. It is recorded that the Serbian monks of that monastery played a very prominent part in the defense of the city againt the piratic Normans from Sicily in 1185, before Sava came to the Holy Mountain. Sava restored that monastery, endowed it, and stayed in it whenever he was in Thessalonika. It was also a station for all the monks of Hilandar.

Traveling on mules with his companion monks, Sava entered the city through the eastern gate. He first paid a visit to the Metropolitan of Thessalonika, Constantine, where he again met Bishop Nicholas, who had ordained him. This bishop enthusiastically described the new Serbian monastery on the Holy Mountain to the Metropolitan, praising Simeon and Sava as true men of God. He spoke of the miracle with the body of Simeon, and of the works and charity of Sava. The Metropolitan looked at the young priest with awe and received him with great friendliness. He asked Sava to participate with him in the church service in the cathedral. At the Liturgy, the Metropolitan made Sava an Archimandrite. Sava thanked them and returned to Philocalos. There he wrote a letter to Stefan, in which he described all that happened at the memorial service for their father in Hilandar. He sent him the flask of the oil as well. All this done, Sava returned with his sojourners to the Holy Mountain with a higher ecclesiastic rank, but deeper humility in his heart before the Lord.

CHAPTER 15

BROTHER AGAINST BROTHER

There is a healthy social principle which makes for peace and happiness among men. It is expressed in St. Paul's words: "Outdo one another in showing honor" (Rom 12:10). Simeon and Sava strictly followed this principle. Simeon regarded Sava as above him, and Sava considered Simeon to be greater than himself. Each one did all in his power to make the other greater and more glorious; each one served the other on the path of salvation. Upon this positive and evangelic principle the Holy Mountain had been founded in its very beginning.

There is on the other hand an anti-social principle of egotism and self-glory which inevitably turns human society, families, nations, or empires into disorder, chaos and misery. This unholy principle prevailed between the two royal brothers in Serbia after the death of their father, St Simeon. The guilt certainly was Vukan's. While his father and his brother on the Holy Mountain made superhuman efforts to save their souls, he did whatever he could to lose his soul.

Dissatisfied with his subordinate position ever since his younger brother Stefan had been appointed Grand Zupan by their father, Nemanja, in Ras, Vukan planned vengeance and subversion. His wife, who had belonged to the Roman Catholic Church, supported his sinister plans. Yet he was afraid to revolt against Stefan during Nemanja's lifetime, although Nemanja was only a monk. He might have remembered what the Bulgarian Tsar Boris, as a monk, did against his self-willed son and successor, Vladimir, when this prodigal son turned back to paganism. Boris put a sword on the belt over his monastic garb, rushed to the capital, made his son blind and shut him up in jail, and then restored order in the state and hurried back to the monastery. Why should Nemanja-Simeon not do the same with his rebel son? So mused Vukan, and waited.

Soon after Simeon's death, however, Prince Vukan put his plans into operation. With a hired mercenary army he attacked Stefan. Though repulsed several times by the Grand Zupan, he repeated his vigorous attacks until he succeeded, with the support of foreigners, the Hungarians. After defeating Stefan and driving him out of the country, Vukan wanted to become a crowned king. He asked for a royal crown from the Pope, Innocent II, who in those days could dispose of royal crowns. He vowed allegiance to the papal church. The Pope sent him a crown, to be brought by a Hungarian archbishop, who also received a papal order to make all the Serbian people Roman Catholics. This was not agreeable to Emeric (Imry), King of Hungary, who himself claimed the title of the King of the Serbs, although he was an ally of Vukan in fighting Stefan. King Emeric therefore did not permit the papal legate to go on his mission to Vukan. Shortly, thereafter, Emeric became involved in a fierce fight with his brother Andreas. In this fight Emeric died and Andreas took the throne of Hungary. This new king, more ambitious than this brother, definitely prevented the papal legate from carrying out his mission among the Serbs. Meanwhile, Stefan, seeing Hungary, Vukan's ally, so crippled through its internal struggle, struck vigorously against Vukan, succeeding in driving him down to the Adriatic coast and regaining his throne and all of the dominion. This happened in 1204.

These four years of fratricidal struggle had left the Serbian land devastated, the economy ruined, the population reduced, its strength diminished, and the fields uncultivated. Because of disorder, insecurity, and starvation, a great number of Serbs emigrated to foreign countries.

In those days, struggles between brothers seem to have been widespread, like epidemics in the world. This was true not only in Serbia and Hungary, but also in Bulgaria and Byzantium. In Buglaria three brothers were constantly at each other's throats: Assen, Peter and John. The first two were assassinated, and John called "Kalojan"—John the Faithful—vested himself in the title of Tsar of Bulgaria.

Byzantium fared worst of all. There too we find a fratricidal struggle which finally brought the Empire under the yoke of the most inhuman of all the conquerors of Constantinople. They were the arrogant Latin soldiers of the Fourth Crusade.

In the short span of about twenty years, six emperors in Constantinople succeeded each other, and not one of them died a natural death. The Christian people of the capital therefore expected God's punishment for these assassinations, but through the infidel Turks of Asia rather than from the Christians of Europe. The terrible blow, however, came from the West and not from the East. It came like a blizzard, during the rule of the Emperor Alexios III Angelos, the father-in-law of the Serbian Grand Župan Stefan, and continued under the short reigns of his successors, Alexios IV Angelos, and Alexios V Ducas. After some feeble resistance Alexios III fled, and later Alexios IV was strangled by the Latins. Alexios Ducas, an intrepid fighter, as a prisoner, was hurled down from a statue one hundred and fifty feet high. After that, the Crusaders, who called themselves Christians, on the first day of the occupation of the Holy City of Eastern Christendom, massacred four thousand Christians although they were on the way to liberate Christians from the Muslim oppression. What an irony! They pillaged and sacked the city of Constantinople, plundered every house, and stripped Saint Sophia and other churches of all their golden vessels, crosses, vestments, ikons and lamps. Their priests eagerly collected the coffins and relics of the saints to carry them to Rome. The official edifices and museums were quickly left empty and bare. A harlot of the street was put on the patriarchal throne in Saint Sophia. After being vested in the patriarchal vestments, she was asked to sing vulgar songs. All western historians extensively but with shame describe the unspeakable atrocities of the Crusaders. And the

Greek chroniclers wrote that "The Franks behaved incomparably worse than the Saracens, for when a town surrendered, the infidels, at any rate, respected the churches and the women. But the bloodthirsty, wild and blind Doge of Venice, Errico Dandolo, took full revenge on the Greeks." Then Pope Innocent sent a Latin archbishop to replace the harlot in the seat of the most illustrious Orthodox Patriarch of the East.

In the face of all these horrible events, both Stefan and Vukan wished to bring about a permanent reconciliation. They asked their youngest brother Sava to come, with the body of their father in order to restore a stable peace between them.

The Crusaders, however, lacking all respect for any of God's sanctuaries under heaven, made frequent intrusions into the Holy Mountain with intentions to steal, to plunder, to desecrate, and to kill. They threatened the independence and peace of the Holy Mountain. They were eager for gold, even if they lost their souls. The liberation of the Holy Land was only a pretense.

Sava pondered and hesitated. He had by then two hundred monks in Hilandar. If he left them alone, he feared they might disperse for dread of the Crusaders. If he stayed in Hilandar, however, the peace between his brothers in Serbia and the cohesion of the Serbian people might be ruined.

He was between two fires, and he had to decide. He hurried to the House of Silence to pray and to ask for God's infallible guidance.

CHAPTER 16

THE PEACEMAKER

Finally, Sava decided to return to Serbia. He did so with a heavy heart. Twenty years had passed since he as a youth had retired from the world and found a spiritual refuge in the Holy Mountain. Although a foreign land, it was dearer to his heart even than the country of his ancestors. But he was not a man to please himself, but rather one who always did what pleased God. He remembered Christ's words: "Blessed are the peacemakers," and he also remembered his promise to his father that he would transfer his body to Serbia. So he gathered all his strength to wade again through the tumultuous waves of the world. Only for a short time, as he thought.

When the tomb of St. Simeon was opened, they found his body preserved, whole and undecomposed, eight years after his death. Sava invited a group of the best known Fathers of the Holy Mountain to go with him. They took the coffin with the body and and started the weary journey to Serbia.

Being informed beforehand, the Grand Župan Stefan went out to meet Sava at the Greek frontier. He was escorted by his sons, by the Bishop of Ras with numerous clergy, noblemen and state dignitaries. The brothers embraced each other with tenderness and tears. Then Stefan bowed before Sava and before the coffin of his father. He also bowed deep before Sava's venerable companions, kissed their hands and asked for their blessing. The Fathers of the Holy Mountain, used to such humility among themselves, were surprised to discover it in a secular potentate. From the very first they admired and loved Stefan, the elder brother of their guide, Sava. The guards of the Grand Župan followed the example of their Lord.

After resting a while, they moved slowly in procession, with the clergy chanting a litany, the bells ringing, the incense burning, and the ever-increasing crowd of people singing and crying for joy. For their former powerful lord and ruler Nemanja, under whom they had enjoyed peace and abundance, was now returning to them as a powerful saint, only to find them disturbed and impoverished because of the brothers' strife. They were now full of great expectations. Though the old man was bodily dead, he was alive as a mighty saint, mightier now than when he had left them alive. The saints are always mightier than kings and emperors. Besides, there was his marvelous son, about whose saintly life and wondrous works legends had circulated among the Serbs for many years. Thus the people were perlexed as to whom to admire more, and to whom to render greater homage—to the father or to the son? They had both come back together as a precious treasure to enrich their country, and as a blessing from God.

At the gate of Studenica, the procession was met by the Reverend Dionisije, the first superior of the monastery whom Nemanja had appointed. After a memorial service, the glorified body of Saint Simeon was buried in the tomb of marble which the saint had prepared for himself at the time he built Studenica. Prince Vukan, with his sons and grandsons, was also present. He greeted Sava with great respect, not as his brother, but as his spiritual father and lord.

After a short rest, Sava proceeded to perform solemn liturgies every day, with hearty prayers for repentance and the increase of brotherly love between the brothers. At every liturgy he preached strong sermons, warning, instructing, and consoling the great and the small. The Fathers of the Holy Mountain assisted in these services. They were impressed by the greatness and the beauty of the marble church of Studenica, and charmed by the kindness and hospitality of the Serbian monks and people. By Sava's wish they talked to the Serbian monks on every occasion of a holy life leading to eternal salvation and bliss. So they stayed in Studenica until the next annual celebration of St Simeon's day.

Meanwhile, Sava talked to his brothers, Stefan and Vukan, in private. A biographer describes the results of those talks: "Through Sava's presence," says he, "the two brothers became united in great love." Listening to the saint, Vukan felt ashamed of himself, because he had trespassed against their father's orders. He said, however, that his rebellion had not been by his own will, but by the instigation of dignitaries at his court. Thereafter hostilities ceased among the brothers, and their followers ceased quarreling.

The peace established among the brothers was strengthened even more on St Simeon's day, when the holy oil again began to flow from the body of the Saint, in Studenica as it had in Hilandar. This was the fruit of Sava's incessant prayers to God: "O God, my Savior, I humbly pray to Thee, glorify this Thy saint in the West, in his native land, as Thou has glorified him in the East, on the Holy Mountain. Inasmuch as Thou hast glorified him in a foreign land, do Thou glorify him even more in our own land. Thereby the faith of these people will be confirmed by a miracle and these men, whom I have brought with me from the East will know that we in the West too are true servants of the Holy Trinity. With hope in Thee, I have brought these men with me. Put me not to shame in my expectations."

So prayed Sava, and after he had finished his prayer, the oil began to flow. A sweet odor filled the great church. The people were startled and the monks of the Holy Mountain lifted their voices to praise the Lord, just as they had done in Hilandar when the miracle first happened before their eyes. The people prostrated themselves in the church. Stefan and Vukan, weeping, embraced each other. The sick were quickly brought to be sprinkled with the oil, to become whole. Then a unanimous praise was sung. Great festivities followed for several days while people came running from all directions to see the wonder and to praise God and St Simeon.

After the celebration, the Fathers of the Holy Mountain

wanted to go home. Sava wished to return with them, but Stefan implored him to stay. "Do not leave us at this moment, O saintly Father, but remain with us in order to establish peace and order with good laws among the people of thy fatherland. For God has sent you, I believe, to finish what our venerable father left unfinished. And I will be obedient to you as your servant." Sava was unable to oppose this wise appeal. So the monks had to leave without him. They were presented with rich gifts by the Grand Župan and by Sava, as well as by many other persons. After this they took leave, and being escorted to the frontier by a guard of honor, went in peace to the Holy Mountain.

Then all the Serbian people greatly feared the Lord and Sava.

CHAPTER 17

BY DEEDS AND WORDS

In Serbia, as in Byzantium, an Emperor or King who had built a monastery had the right, if he so wished, to appoint a superior of that monastery. Nemanja used that right in Studenica, his chief votive church, and stipulated in his Rule of Studenica that this right belonged to his successor of the dynasty. According to this inherited right, Stefan appointed Archimandrite Sava the superior of Studenica, not only because he was the fittest for that post but most probably because he wanted to bind him closer to Serbia. Before long, however, Sava overcame his longing for the Holy Mountain by plunging into activity. The new environment soon became familiar to him.

First of all, he must have been fascinated by the unsurpassed beauty of the white marble church in the evergreen pine forest. He saw it now for the first time, for his father had built it some years after he had left Serbia. No such church existed on the Holy Mountain. Studenica was larger and higher than Hilandar, of a mixed Byzantino-Dalmatian style. Besides, it had been richly endowed by Nemanja and was able to maintain a large brotherhood. Then last but not least, his holy father was there with him, living, wonderworking, and lovingly watching and guiding from the other world. The whole white church stood before him as a beautiful body which breathed the spirit and holiness of Saint Simeon. Thus the presence of his father took the place for him of the Holy Mountain.

Sava speedily copied his Hilandar's Typicon or Rule, for Studenica, with some slight changes. He drew a great number of novices, both from the Serbian nobility and the peasantry, who desired the monastic way of life. He kept in Studenica several of the distinguished Serbian Fathers from the Holy Mountain to help him in training a new generation of monks, as well as for teaching, hearing confessions, writing and multiplying books, and painting church walls and ikons. He set the discipline for all the inhabitants of the monastery, as well as for guests and visitors. It was not like the discipline of a military camp, but that of God's spiritual family. He put the management in order, and he raised to the highest level the production of food, wine, honey, fish and livestock, in order not only to sustain hundreds of monks, but also thousands of pilgrims, schoolboys, visitors, and the sick. Thus Studenica soon became the most attractive sanctuary of the nation. Nothing in the world attracts human souls so irresistibly as genuine sanctity. People from all corners of the state flocked to Studenica to worship, to learn, to see miracles, to be relieved of their sins and be healed, to look upon the face of the Prince-monk Sava, to attend his inspiring liturgies, to hear his words, to receive from his hands Holy Communion and blessings, to be anointed with the oil of St Simeon. Multitudes came also to see something that is quite uncommon—how even the rich can enter the Kingdom of Heaven.

Sava had to provide food and lodging for all who came, as well as to minister to them spiritually. This he did quietly as a monk, and quickly as a servant.

He built additional large buildings around the monastery for the monks and their workshops, as well as for housing. He also built several smaller churches in the fields and vineyards, distant from the monastery, for the use of the monks working in those places, and for the surrounding population. These churches in turn built refuges for the monks as well as storage buildings. Most of these are now lying in ruins due to the centuries-long oppressive rule of the Turks.

Thus, Sava, first put his own house in excellent order, according to the Apostolic recommendation (I Tim. 3:4-5), and then he expanded his nation-wide activities to the furthest ends of the Serbian land from Studenica as a radiating center. He went out as a sower who sowed good seed into the souls of men. He preached the Gospel of Christ, the right way of believing, the right way of feeling, the right way of doing, the holy way leading to the Kingdom of Heaven. He called the people to repentance. He explained that sin was the only barrier between man and God, between man and man's happiness. He urged everyone to remove that barrier in order to see the light and enjoy happiness. He taught the people how to pray and fast and be clean and charitable. He stressed the importance of Baptism, Holy Communion and other great mysteries necessary to purify, feed and fortify the soul and body. He warned against the heretics who, like the Bogomils, denied the sacraments or, like the Roman Catholics, administered them incorrectly. He instituted good Christian customs instead of heathen ones, expounded the laws and regulations of the Orthodox Church, told the people biblical stories and the stories of the great Christian saints and martyrs. He described the life of the monks of the Holy Mountain and their almost superhuman efforts for the sake of their souls, and for the sake of Christ's love. He never failed to mention his father Saint Simeon and God's miracles on and through him. He continued to build churches everywhere, churches of stone or of wood. In some places he erected wooden crosses instead of a church.

The people felt in Sava's person a true friend and shepherd. They readily believed and obeyed him because they saw him doing what he was teaching. "The people were fed by his words as by honey." They loved his simplicity and his sincerity. For he went among the plain people with simplicity as one of them and yet with unobtrusive superiority of an apostle. Moreover God confirmed him as His own messenger by many miracles he wrought healing the sick by prayers.

Indeed, we can say of Sava: "A great light appeared in the darkness of ignorance and confusion in the country of the Serbs."

CHAPTER 18

ANOTHER HOUSE OF

The most striking place near Studenica, but to the north of it, is called "Nemanja's Tower." To reach it you must walk up the rapid, murmuring Studenica River. On your left you will see springs of water and the quarry of white marble which Nemanja used to build his great church. A little further, as you pass through the forest, you may step down to the brink of the river to drink the sparkling mineral water, which is very healthful and refreshing. After about an hour of walking, you cross the river over a narrow wooden bridge and turn to your left to climb a hill. You proceed first through bushes with a few small trees until you get to the boundary of a sacred ground with a fine shade forest, where the trees are safe from a stranger's ax and it would be a sacrilege to eat meat. Such is the rule of St. Sava, everyone will tell you. For that forest and ground belong to his House of Silence, or Postnica. For another hour you walk through the forest until suddenly an inviting green glen appears before you. You cross a tiny silvery brook—there you are in Lower Postnica—from which you have to climb for about half an hour to Upper Postnica. In Lower Postnica you will be welcomed by two or three monks of Studenica brotherhood. In their simple quarters they will show you a beautiful small chapel, in which they strictly keep the prayer rule prescribed by Saint Sava. The brothers will receive you very kindly, but only one of them will answer your questions. The questions exhibiting too much curiosity, however, they will pass over in silence.

Now you walk up a steep mount through a forest of fir trees. Suddenly you find yourself over a precipice. On your right hand stands a high wall of monolithic rock, through which a path has been cut no wider in places than half a yard. On your

. you will see an almost perpendicular slope covered with ıabs of rocks as big as huts, lying in disorder, cast there as if by some titans in battle. At the bottom of this terrific panorama roars the Studenica river. Those with weak nerves turn back to avoid dizziness and loss of balance. At the end you reach a narrow opening in a half-circle. And there you find Saint Sava's Upper Postnica. As a swallow's nest perches on a cliff, there stands a structure of stone and oak beams, now half in ruins. Under that structure there is a well with a little water, which is taken to the sick.

Who could ever foresee that a royal prince of Serbia would choose this frightening precipice for his abode in preference to court life? Sava chose it for his periodic retreats while in Serbia, just as he used the Postnica in Karyes while on the Holy Mountain and this not only while he was a monk or the superior of a monastery, but later also when he was archbishop. He neglected his body in order to make his spirit the Master of it. He denied to the body almost all that it naturally needed. His spiritual reservoirs needed to be replenished. Postnica served Sava as a reservoir to replenish his spirit. He had been too long and too much among the people, traveling, preaching, listening, correcting, working, building. He needed a direct and undisturbed contact with God, to have his spirit touched with God's Spirit. Sava's love for Christ urged him to solitude, as a lover seeks to be alone with his beloved. What he did in his isolation is known to God alone. We presume he did what he had done in his first House of Silence at Karyes. He endeavored to substitute the mind and life of Christ for his own, in accordance with the word of the Apostle: "It is no longer I who live, but Christ lives in me" (Gal 2:20). To live Christ's life, to think Christ's thoughts, to have Christ's love, to do Christ's will, to be like Christ in every respect—this was the aim of all the spiritual exercises of the Desert Fathers of the East. And there is no doubt that that was also Sava's aim in his place of retreat.

We can hardly suppose that Sava went to the retreat in Postnica every Lent, as the great hermits of the Desert did, but he went whenever it was possible. In Serbia he could not be a mere hermit. God sent him to work among the people and for the people. In him the East and the West met in astonishing harmony. He was prone to deep meditation like an Oriental, and vigorous in action like an Occidental. Both of these dispositions, or talents, he developed to perfection. Both were grounded in his great spiritual power.

After the end of his retreat Sava, transfigured as it were, would return to Studenica to gladden and fortify the whole brotherhood with his presence. Then again he would proceed on his journeys all over the country to preach, teach, build, and work among the Serbian people as before.

That was Sava's life year in and year out, until one day he went with a proposal to his illustrious brother, the Grand Župan, to build a great new monastery in the place called Žiča. He had in mind far-reaching plans, only a part of which he confided to his brother. Stefan, convinced by Sava's arguments gladly consented to build a monastery of his own.

CHAPTER 19

A VICTORY WITHOUT A SWORD

In those days, the rulers of nations used to change allies and enemies more quickly than in our days. Sava's chief vocation was to enlighten his people with the right faith and to save them from ignorance and vice. Although he was assisted by a number of his disciples from Hilandar and Studenica, his time was entirely taken up with this work. Besides, he was often called to take upon himself the troublesome work of his brother, the Grand Župan.

Once he had to avert a serious peril endangering the independence of Serbia. Where a great armed force was needed to fight an aggressive Bulgarian prince, he decided to go along with his pastoral staff to oppose the hostile army. The threat came from a certain Prince Strez, a relative and a vassal of the Bulgarian King Kalojan. His princedom was southeast of the Vardar river. He was an audacious and reckless person. His ambitions were greater than his mind and much greater than his honesty. But as long as the terrible King Kalojan was alive, he dared not stir against him.

However, as soon as Kalojan met a sudden death at the siege of Thessalonika, Strez rebelled against Borillo, the nephew and successor of Kalojan. He struck quickly and brought into his subjection nearly half of the Bulgarian kingdom. The Serbian Župan supported Strez in his endeavors. King Borillo several times requested Stefan to withdraw his support of the rebellious prince. Stefan, however, must have calculated that Strez would be a less dangerous neighbor than Borillo. Therefore even Borillo's last, angry demand of Stefan to deliver Strez to him "to be burnt or cut in pieces" remained to no avail. For Strez implored Stefan not to abandon him, promising more than his character allowed him to fulfill. Instead of complying with the wish of the Bulgarian King, Stefan made an alliance with Strez, taking him as a vassal under his protection. Both pledged mutual loyalty and made a vow, with their hands upon the Gospel, of true brotherhood. Borillo alone was unable to use force against Stefan and Strez. Among other problems he had suffered a great defeat by the Latin Emperor Henry at Plovidv (1208).

In those days, however, a marriage helped when everything else failed. The defeated King of Bulgaria gave members of his family in marriage to the Latin Emperor. Thus yesterday's foes became today's friends, and not only friends, but military allies as well. With their combined forces they invaded Serbia and came near to the city of Niš. But now the military situation was reversed. One night the Bulgarian and Latin armies saw in the air an apparition of Saint Simeon threatening them furiously. Shivering with terror, the army retreated in a hasty flight homeward.

Some time after this lost war, the allies tried to bribe Strez and arouse him against Stefan. They tempted him with a promise of all the Serbian land he might be successful in conquering. Strez's conscience could not resist such a temptation. He consented, quickly gathered a large army and prepared for a sudden strike against Serbia.

Stefan was informed of the evil intentions of his enemy to make war against him. He sent him a warning, then another and then a third. But Strez remained obstinate. Finally, the Serbs too raised an army to defend their country.

Thereupon, Sava offered to go himself to Strez to stop him in the name of Christ. With the approval of his brother Stefan, he went with a few companions to Prosek, the residence of the treacherous prince. Prosek was a narrow gorge between high rocks through which the Vardar River flows. Upon a cliff 1200 feet high, Strez had built a citadel in which he resided. There he had also a theater adjacent to his abode, and at an end of the theater a spacious veranda overhanging the river. There he and his companions lived a riotous life, feasting and drinking all the time. He always kept a number of captives in jail, and he would entertain his banqueting friends by hurling some of the poor captives from the high veranda down into the river. He would shout as they hurtled downwards: "Take care that your sheepskin coat doesn't get wet!" Stefan had heard of cruelties by his outlaw ally and rebuked him very sharply, but in vain.

This was the man to whom Sava came as a peacemaker. On his way, he saw troops of soldiers in great number. Strez, however, received Sava with all signs of great respect and feigned friendship. Sava first used gentle language, speaking to his host of Christian faith and the love to which we all are pledged by baptism, of the honesty and sincerity of Christian rulers in dealing with each other, of the horrors of wars and bloodshed among Christ's followers, of Stefan's deepest desire to live in peace with his rebellious neighbor, and so forth. It was all in vain. The more the saint pleaded with Strez, the more this man become intractable and even enraged. He was not accustomed to kind words, only to slander or flattery. He probably needed a lion tamer with a whip, not a saint to tame him. At the end of their talk, Sava changed his form of speech and threatened the rebel with God's justice and with punishment for perjury and bloodshed. These threatening words silenced Strez, but did not change his mind. So Sava left the citadel and went to his tent outside of Prosek.

It was a dark night. Sava resorted to prayer as usual. What is impossible for men is possible for God. He did not stop praying for hours. Suddenly, after midnight, the news came that Strez was dead. Dying in his castle, he cried: "Quick, bring me Sava! A young man sent by Sava has pierced my heart with a sword. Sava, Sava, quick!" Of course, all the sober men in the castle thought that it was an angel of God who had struck him. As soon as the news of the tyrant's death became known, the army dispersed, and at dawn the military camp was empty.

Sava returned home sad and silent, for although he had saved his country, he could not bring Strez to repentance to save his soul. Stefan embraced his brother, crying for joy and gratitude, but Sava was silent and mournful for the loss of a human soul! After this Sava stood before the Serbian army and delivered a speech in which he said: "Brothers, the Lord has delivered us without any loss of arms, horses or manpower, by killing our adversary. The Lord alone has done this, through the intercession of the Holy Virgin and our father Saint Simeon. Strez died because of his haughtiness and cruelty toward his fellow men, because of his perjury and his lack of fear of God. Therefore, live in fear of the Almighty God, who ceaselessly looks down and sees all our deeds both good and shameful. Do not make war except in defense of God's justice. No evil shall ever befall you if you are steady and ready to do what pleases God, in whom never cease to have confidence."

Thereafter Serbia enjoyed peace for a long time, thanks to Sava. And Sava with Stefan started to build the monastery of Žiča.

CHAPTER 20

THE WORKER AND
THE WONDERWORKER

Do more than you are expected to do, and you will need no personal recommendation. This is an American saying in business and other circles of practical life. "Receiving a small amount of authority, he created great works," says an ancient biographer of Sava. In other words, being only a priest and not yet a bishop, he did things beyond his ecclesiastic rank.

After he had averted the danger threatening the freedom and independence of the Serbian State from the rapacious Prince Strez, Sava retired to Studenica to continue his constructive work. There in peace he gave himself to writing. He composed "The Life of Saint Simeon," a book of historic value inspired by a glowing filial love. Then he wrote epistles to the brotherhood of Hilandar and many letters to priests and laymen, admonishing, correcting or instructing them. He wrote also to the Serbian princes of Dalmatia and Dukleja, warning them against Latin missionaries, and to those of Hercegovina and Bosnia warning them of the Bogomils; both of these heresies were then active in undermining Orthodoxy in the Balkans. Besides this writing activity, he continued in Studenica to train monks for missionary work and others for parish priesthood. He gathered the village boys on Sundays and taught them to read the sacred books and to write and sing in the church. Also he continued to travel among the people, teaching, preaching and reconciling. But with all this preoccupation, he did not stop building Žiča.

As we have said before, Stefan gladly accepted Sava's proposal to build Žiča. "You know," Sava said to Stefan, "how our father built Studenica, which is a spiritual center, the pride and adornment of our country. You know, too, of all the other wonderful churches he as a Grand Župan built on Serbian soil in order to sanctify that soil and to promote the enlightenment of the people by divine knowledge. It would not be proper that you as a Grand Župan should live and die without leaving to posterity at least one great monastery. Moreover, your country has been much enlarged by the help of God and Saint Simeon. Studenica alone is not enough for the spiritual needs of our enlarged country. We need badly another center too. Besides, you owe to God great gratitude for all your successes in war and in peace. Therefore build Žiča as a visible token of your gratitude to the Almighty.''

Sava had another plan in mind concerning Žiča. He had a vision of the Serbian independent church, of Žiča as the seat of the Serbian archbishop, and as the national sanctuary in which the future Serbian kings should be crowned by the head of the Serbian Church residing there. At this point, Stefan would have shrunk from such a grandiose plan. Such an independent Orthodox Church, existing only in Serbia, would alarm its neighbors, and Stefan would not have been willing to take that step. Sava knew this, and he therefore proceeded cautiously, counting on God and time.

Stefan accepted without hesitation the idea of building a votive church of his own, however. To this end, he gave Sava means and complete authority to choose the place for the new church, to make the plans and to employ competent masons and artisans of every kind. For although he considered himself incompetent for such an undertaking, never having built a church before, he believed that Sava was highly qualified for such work.

Sava chose a place on the right bank of the Ibar River, of which the Studenica River is a tributary, as the Ibar is a tributary of the West Morava River. There, near the mouth of the Ibar River on a low-hill, Žiča was built in accordance with Sava's wish. It lies in the very center of the present Šumadija, on the plain surrounded by forested mountains, and is much more accessible than Studenica. And now Sava set about

vigorously to work on Žiča with the same fervor he had
brought to building Hilandar, but with much greater experience. He gathered the best artisans and masters in stone,
metal, and woodwork from Thessalonika and the Greek
islands. He wanted the best workmen to create the best results.
He himself helped all he could with his brain and his hands, but'
particularly with his constant prayers. A merciful God
answered his prayers with miracles.

Once a day, the Grand Župan came to see what his brother
was doing. It happened that a paralytic had been brought for
alms. Seeing such a helpless sufferer, Sava became very much
distressed. He offered no coins, but took him in his arms, and
with the help of his disciples, brought him into the church, probably into the little church of the Holy Apostles which he had
built quickly for everyday services before he started the great
church. He covered the invalid with his own robe. It was evening. He closed the door and remained alone with the paralytic
inside. Now, bent over the invalid on the floor, he started to
pray and to weep, continuing until morning. At dawn, when
the monks usually gathered outside the church, Sava shouted
to the paralytic: "In the name of our Lord Jesus Christ, I speak
to you, my son, get up and walk!" And, instantly the paralytic
sprang up and walked. Sava then opened the church and let the
man go in strength and joy. The monks and the people marveled, praising God.

The news of this miracle spread like fire over the country.
Nothing in the world stirs people so much as does a miracle.
The consequence was that sick people from everywhere flocked
to Žiča, and Sava continued healing them by prayer, laying on
of hands and anointing them with oil.

Thus the Lord glorified His glorifier and His work, so that
Žiča gained great fame even before its completion, through the
renown of Saint Sava.

CHAPTER 21

SOLITUDE

There are two phrases often repeated in Holy Writ: "Standing before the Lord" and "Seeking the face of the Lord." A monk of the Holy Mountain is taught from the beginning to realize these two precepts in his own life by constant exercises. Therefore every conscientious monk is reluctant to leave the Holy Mountain, to be immersed in the troubled waters of the world, not because he hates the world, but because he does not want to forego or break his practice of standing before the Lord and seeking His face. Even those who were pressed by Emperors and the people to become archbishops or patriarchs opposed it as long as they could; when they finally had to go they went sadly with a heavy heart. As St Arsenius the Great put it: "God knows I love men, but I can't be at the same time with God and with men."

Our Serbian saint refused for a full twenty years to comply with the wishes of his parents and brothers who implored him to return to Serbia from the Holy Mountain. Only after being pressed by circumstances and stimulated through a vision of his father in the House of Silence did he decide to go to his native country for a short time, with the firm intention of returning as quickly as possible. Yet he remained in Serbia for ten years. And though he filled those years with an amazing amount of useful and superhuman activity, to the satisfaction of everyone but himself, nevertheless his craving for the Holy Mountain never left him. His retreats to Upper Postnica could only mitigate this yearning but not kill it. Like all the saints he felt lonely in the wilderness of the world and could have repeated the Psalmist's words: "I have become a stranger to my brethren, and an alien to my mother's sons" (Ps 69:8). The greatest saints must endure the greatest struggles, in which

67

they sometimes too, were given over to despondency, as even the Apostles testify (2 Cor 12:7-9). In those moments the spiritual struggler, conscious of the impotence of the whole world to help him, wants to be left alone. The greater Sava's works became the greater the esteem he earned, the greater loneliness he felt. The world seemed to be a screen between him and his God. "Remembering his first crucified life in the Holy Mountain, he considered himself miserable and lost." Therefore, he decided to go.

Some modern historians conjecture that Sava left Serbia because of his disagreement on some vital matters with his brother. Stefan had divorced his first wife Eudokia, the daughter of the Emperor Alexios Angelos, and for purely political reasons married Anna, the granddaughter of Venetian Doge Enrico Dandolo. This woman was reputedly a zealous Roman Catholic and ambitious, too. She wanted her husband to be a king and the Serbs converted to Roman Catholicism. Her native Venetian Republic could be the mediator in this matter, she suggested to the Pope, who in those days held a monopoly on regal crowns. At that time the Pope was Honorius III. Stefan was certainly in a difficult position, for two Catholic kings, Henry VI of the Latin Kingdom of Constantinople and Andreas II of Hungary, were allied against him. This was, of course, not without the approval of Rome. In such a dangerous situation, Stefan favored his wife's plan and sent a delegation to the Pope, while he himself hurried to meet King Andreas. Both kings had already marched with their armies against Serbia. Stefan met Andreas at Ravni (Cuprija). It is surprising how quickly the Grand Župan came to terms with the Hungarian king, and even became friends with him. Moreover, Andreas promised to intercede with the Latin King Henry to let Serbia alone. And so the Serb and the Hungarian parted as friends. After hearing from Andreas, Henry returned home angry and humiliated. Meanwhile, the Pope swiftly sent a crown to Stefan, who was to be crowned as a Catholic king, but this was never carried out. Sava with all his might opposed and frustrated the cunning plans of his brother's wife. He stood firmly for Orthodoxy as the only true way of salvation for the Serbian people and their freedom. His father too had repudiated his Roman baptism in childhood and had let himself be baptized in the Orthodox Church.

Some modern historians maintain that Sava left Serbia because of his conflict with his brother's court. This is not what the ancient biographers record. On the contrary, they describe most touchingly the scene of the separation of the two. Nevertheless, we think that the modern historians may be right.

With his mind made up to depart, Sava first put everything in order. In Žiča he roofed the great church. In Studenica he exhorted the brothers to keep the Rule and to live in love and in the fear of God. Sava wept at the tomb of his father, asking for his protection and blessing for himself and the Serbian people. Then he went to Ras to bid the Grand Župan, his brother Stefan, farewell. Stefan cried loudly and tried to persuade Sava to remain. "He felt as if his soul was leaving him." Sava consoled his brother by saying: "If God wills it, I may come to you again." Then Stefan handed him a sum of money for his needs and for charity, escorted him to the Greek frontier, and returned home very sad and depressed.

Sava, however, leaving sadness behind, met joy ahead. For he was received on the Holy Mountain with great gladness, and not only by the brotherhood of Hilandar but by the brothers from all of the monasteries who rushed to see him.

Sava was not destined to stay long in Hilandar. After he had surveyed the monastery and had seen what had been done during his absence, and often praying and conversing with the abbot, and the brothers, consoling and praising them all, he left for Postnica, his first House of Silence at Karyes. There he did not feel lonely. For there he stood before the Lord, seeking the face of the Lord. There he continued his usual inner activity undisturbed. But he was also working on other plans, as we shall see.

CHAPTER 22

THE PATHFINDER IN
THE WILDERNESS

It would be impossible for us to love God unless we knew that "he loved us first." Reflecting on his life in solitude, Sava must have found that God indeed loved him first. This knowledge from self-experience made his soul aflame with the love of God. With all his strength he concentrated his love on God, and on God alone. But such a concentration was this time hindered by his memory of Serbia. He could not defend himself from this memory. Like a sudden breeze, it would come to his heart from nowhere, whispering to him in the absolute stillness of his House of Silence; "Think of Serbia! If you love me, help my Serbian people! Continue to help them for my sake! I am with you." This was not the first time that Sava had had visions and had heard voices from the other world. Sava was experienced in discriminating among spirits. He was sure it was God who spoke to him, and not the evil one. He might have repeated Moses' words: "Wherefore have I not found favor in your sight, that you lay the burden of all these people upon me? Have I begotten them, that you should say to me: 'Carry them in your bosom as a nursing father?' Great leaders used to speak boldly to God. Thus the Psalmist cried: "Rouse thyself, why sleepest thou, O Lord? Awake, do not, cast us off forever" (Ps 44:23).

Sava was forced to analyze the Serbian situation. He distinctly saw two negative forces counteracting all his positive efforts and influence. The first was the Roman Church, and the second the Bogomil heresy. Each of them was sufficient to obliterate the Orthodox character of the Serbian people if not checked in time.

The Papal church had deviated from the Christian dogmas, clearly defined by the apostles and Seven Ecumenical Coun-

cils. It had inserted into the Creed an erroneous sentence about
the Holy Spirit. It had diluted the severity of Christian ethics
by lax moral doctrines. It ordered celibacy for all the clergy,
contrary to the fact that the Apostle Peter of the Twelve and
many of the Seventy Apostles had been married men. It exalted
the Pope both in eccelesiastic and secular authority to the position of an absolute ruler. A semi-religious and semi-military
organization, it used all means to gain world dominion. To
bring the Balkan peoples into the fold of Rome, by cross or by
sword, has been the desired goal of the popes for over a thousand years, and the Serbian Orthodox people have been
throughout this period the first bulwark against that aggressive
goal.

In Sava's time, the Orthodox Balkans were in the grip of
Latinism more than ever before. The Fourth Crusade went
with the Pope's blessing, not to liberate Jerusalem, but to
enslave the Orthodox Christians in Constantinople. A Roman
Patriarch was set up in the capital of Orthodox Christendom,
another in Bulgaria during the reign of Kalojan. A Latin
Kingdom was established also in Thessalonika, and another in
Greece. In the north the Roman Catholic kings were often in-
cited by the Vatican to fight and conquer Serbia so that it could
be Romanized. Now what could the Grand Župan do alone?
And how long could the Serbian people resist all of these odds,
in addition to sharp attacks from every direction, without a
strongly organized Orthodox Church? Every Christian nation
had a spiritual head but the Serbs. The Ecumenical Patriarch
lived in exile in Asia. Stefan stood alone as the secular ruler
without a strong ecclesiastic authority supporting him. He
alone was unable to stand the pressure effectively for long. He
needed a Serbian archbishop and an independent national
church with national clergy.

The second menacing force, not external but internal, was
the Bogomils. They threatened both the Church and the state
with disruption. According to their Manichean theory, God
created only the world of spirits, but the devil created mat-

ter, material bodies, and the material world generally. Consequently, all material things are evil and come from the evil one, and as such ought to be shunned. They kept as a law total abstinence from meat and wine and they denied marriage. They rejected the Old Testament and read only the Psalms and the New Testament. They rejected also the church hierarchy, baptism, Holy Communion and all the sacraments, the veneration of church buildings, ikons, crosses, relics, liturgies, miracles and church canons, as well as all the institutions of the state. They believed that all these came from the devil, being connected with matter. They attracted masses of people by their asceticism, which has always appealed to people in the East. This faith had originated in Asia Minor. Driven from there, they appeared in Thrace and Bulgaria. Here their leader was a certain priest Pope Bogomil, from whom the movement in the Balkans derived the name "Bogomils." When they were persecuted in Bulgaria, they migrated to central Serbia, and were driven by Nemanja into Bosnia. There they became deeply rooted because they reformed many of their traditional teachings; they permitted meat, wine and marriage, and built monasteries, settling into the society. At one time they were so popular that a number of princes and lords in Bosnia and Hercegovina became their adherents and protectors. Some Catholic bishops were converted to Bogomilism. The Pope ordered Crusades against them with violent persecutions, first in Bosnia and later in southern France, where they were called Albigensians and Cathari. But in spite of all these cruel persecutions, they survived for several centuries.

Sava believed that persuasion, not violence, should be used to get rid of the Bogomils. This seems to be the only point in which he was not in agreement with his father Nemanja. But who was going to persuade and teach the Bogomils and convert them to the right faith? Certainly not the two Greek bishops in Serbia, or the priests under them. Here again Sava was fully convinced that the most urgent need of his people was a strongly organized, national, independent church with an archbishop and well-educated clergy of Serbian origin.

Such thoughts disturbed Sava in his isolation in the House of Silence. Sava was also disturbed by reports of disorder in Orthodoxy in general. Bulgaria was constantly vacillating between the Orthodox and Roman Churches. The King of Bulgaria formally recognized the Pope, as he himself had been converted to the Roman Church and was under obligation to convert all the Bulgarian people to the Roman Catholic faith. Because of the Latin Rule, the Church of Constantinople was split into three administrative centers. The lawful Patriarch resided in Nicaea in Asia Minor, the Kingdom of Trebizond had its own church head, and the western kingdom of Epiros recognized the Archbishop of Ohrida. The Orthodox patriarchates in Asia and Africa were under the Muslim Sultans. The churches in Rumania and Russia were in a transitory, chaotic condition. There could be no cooperation, and therefore there was distressing weakness everywhere.

Surveying the deplorable position of the Orthodox Church as a whole, Sava sorrowfully implored God to show him the true path for the constructive unity of the Orthodox world and the good will and co-operation of all heads of the divided church.

The Pathseeker became the Pathfinder as well.

CHAPTER 23

A NARRATIVE OF STRANGE EVENTS

The communion of saints has always been understood in the Christian Church in a universal sense as the communion of the Church visible and the Church invisible. The saints in the body are the believers and the bodiless saints are those who behold the glory of Christ, the Savior. The difference between them is not in kind but in degree of vision and power.

Saint Simeon, as a monk on earth, was the spiritual son of Sava, but after his death and glorification, when numbered with the saints in the heavenly Church, he became the spiritual father and protecting spirit of Sava. The physical relationship in the physical world during life does not change, but when the two worlds are taken into account, those relationships do change. Two main proofs of Simeon's sainthood in heaven were the flowing of the oil from his body, the healing oil which helped many sick persons, and the miracles by which he had saved the Serbian people from their aggressive foes. There were countless miracles of the healing of the sick by the oil flowing from his body. For as long as Sava remained in Serbia, the oil never stopped flowing. But as soon as Sava left Serbia, something happened which was interpreted to mean that the soul of St Simeon had left too and had gone with Sava.

It came to pass one day, when Sava was in Hilandar after the end of his retreat in the House of Silence, busy as usual, that the watchman from the tower gave the alert. "A group of horsemen are nearing the monastery from the seacost," said he. Quickly the order was given to ring the special bell as a signal of approaching danger, calling all the brothers outside the walls to rush in and to shut the gate. For in those days the monks in the dominion of the Holy Virgin lived in constant anticipation of Latin freebooters, plunderers and killers. After the order had been carried out and the gate shut, the brothers stood in ardent prayer, ready for whatever might happen. And then in the deadly stillness, the watchman's voice was heard, and the brothers listened breathlessly. They heard him talking in Serbian to the strangers beyond the wall. A little after that he shouted down from the tower: "Messengers of the Grand Župan, open the gate!"

The Serbian cavaliers entered the sacred precincts of Hilandar, going first to the church, escorted by a file of monks. After prayer, Sava took them up to the reception room. "All is well in Serbia and the Grand Župan sends his greetings," said they, and handed to Sava Stefan's letter. The letter read as follows: "After Your Reverence left us, my lord, our father Simeon, hid his face from us. His oil ceased to flow. The wonders of healing, by which we had been strengthened and consoled, have not been seen since. We prayed much, appealing to his merciful paternal heart, but he did not want to listen to us. Whether this happened to us because of our sins, or because you are not with us to cleanse us from our sins, we do not know. Therefore, I, your unworthy brother implore you, heed my tears and be merciful. Come and pray with authority to our holy father Simeon to let the wonderful oil flow from his sacred relics by the Holy Spirit as before, and thereby strengthen and gladden us, his servants."

This touching appeal, however, did not move Sava very much. Even when he was a boy of seventeen, he had not followed the emotional calls of his parents, and he would be even less moved now, nearing fifty, to follow his brother's appeal to return home. He was not indifferent to Stefan's appeal, however. The messengers added much by explaining the anguish of the Grand Župan and the dissatisfaction of the people. The masses of people thought that Sava had left their country and that St Simeon had withheld oil because of some guilt of Stefan's. The king's enemies were busy in stirring the people against him, so he was in an awkward position.

Sava fully realized the situation, and he was ready to meet his brother's wish halfway. He would help him for now by prayer, but not by returning home. He already had in his mind a complete plan for helping the Serbian people more fundamentally and permanently. Therefore, he wrote two letters— one to their father St Simeon and the other to his brother Stefan.

It may seem strange to write a letter to a dead person as Sava did. For the supernatural and the natural are not so sharply separated in the consciousness of a visionary believer as they are for those of little faith. Several such cases were recorded in church history. In his letter to St. Simeon, Sava wrote: "O Saint Simeon, as God commands and as we implore you, overlook our trespasses and disobedience toward you. For whatever we are, we are your children. Therefore make the oil flow again from your body in the tomb as before, to the joy and relief of all your people, who are now in great mourning." He wrote the second letter to Stefan, consoling and encouraging him. In this letter, Sava wrote to his brother of his great plan to make the Serbian Church independent.

The letters were sent with a Hilandar brother Ilarion, a highly venerated hieromonk. When he had arrived with messengers in Serbia, Ilarion handed one letter to the Grand Župan and the other he said would be opened and read in Studenica. In this monastery Stefan had assembled a great number of his courtiers, ministers and generals, and a multitude of people following them, all curious to see what message was brought from Sava. After solemn liturgy, Ilarion came in a procession to the tomb of St Simeon, opened Sava's letter and read it loudly. All those present shivered upon hearing a living man writing to one dead. After the reading was finished, a noise was heard, like that of falling water. And behold, the oil again began to flow from the tomb, and not from the tomb alone, but also from the fresco picture of the Saint above the tomb. After a momentary fear and amazement, inexpressible joy filled the hearts of all those present.

Then Stefan wrote a letter of gratitude to Sava. In this letter he also expressed his full approval of Sava's great plan concerning the independence of the Serbian Church, adding a sufficient sum of money for Sava's future travels, and with honors and gifts saw Father Ilarion off to the Holy Mountain.

SAVA THE ARCHBISHOP

The life of our saint has revealed that he was wise in planning and persistent in executing. After almost two years of praying and planning in the tranquility of the Holy Mountain, he boarded a ship and with a few selected monks sailed from Hilandar eastward, not to Constantinople, but to Asia Minor, for a Latin King and a Roman Catholic Patriarch were still ruling in Constantinople. The Orthodox Emperor and the Orthodox Patriarch resided in Nicaea, Asia Minor.

Theodore Laskaris was the Emperor and Manuel Sarantenus the Patriarch. This Theodore was not a member of any of the imperial dynasties of Byzantium, except that was the son-in-law of the former Emperor Alexius III. Thus he did not inherit the imperial crown, he earned it. In the defense of Constantinople, he had fought as a general against the Latins under two emperors, his father-in-law and Alexius Ducas. He fought like a lion to the very last moment. Even when he saw one emperor after another abandon the capital he continued to fight to the end. The battle ended, and so did Constantinople's freedom, when he retreated before overwhelming foes. He retired to Asia Minor in order to continue the fight now against two sets of enemies— the Latins on one side and the Turks on the other. Once he gained such a crushing victory over the Latin army at Brussa, led by Henry of Flanders, the Latins never again dared cross the Sea of Marmara during his lifetime. Then he defeated in battle the Seljuk Turks under the Sultan Kaikhosru. When this Sultan challenged the Christians to a duel, Laskaris courageously went in person and killed the challenger. After these great victories, Theodore Laskaris was crowned Emperor of Byzantium in Nicaea in 1206, gloriously upholding the flag of Constantine the Great, and ruling undisturbed until the end of his life.

The emperor was glad to see Sava, partly because they were slightly related; the empress and Stefan's first wife had been sisters. Moreover, he had heard stories of the holy lives of Sava and Simeon. Patriarch Manuel rejoiced in meeting the princely monk, about whom he had heard so many stories. Thus the reception in Nicaea was indeed dignified and cordial.

Sava, on the other hand, felt fortunate to be in Nicaea. Not only was this city beautiful, contesting for the first rank with two other beautiful cities in Asia Minor, Nicomedia and Brussa, but it was of great importance in the history of Christendom. For here the First Ecumenical Council was held at which the Fathers of the Church, defeating the heretics, composed our Creed, that is, set in a few sentences the truth that God did not send to the world a great man in the person of Jesus of Nazareth, but His unique Son, "light of light, true God of true God," incarnate in the person of Jesus Christ, the Savior of men.

After several days of entertainment, church services, and discussion, Sava stood up before the emperor and the patriarch and told them of the spiritual needs of the Serbian people. He recounted to them of the efforts of his father and his brother in checking the Roman assaults, direct or indirect, upon Orthodox Serbia, and of the influence of the Bogomil sect. He explained that both of these organizations would be rampant in the Balkans as long as the Serbian people, being the forefront of Orthodoxy in the West, stood without their own hierarchy. Therefore it was of extreme and urgent importance to strengthen and vitalize the Serbian church by giving it an archbishop of its own. A well organized and strengthened Church in Serbia would mightily help the normalization of Church affairs in Bulgaria, which was then sadly undermined by Roman Catholicism. Impressed deeply by Sava's lucid explanations, both the emperor and the patriarch gladly accepted his proposal as a very reasonable and appropriate one. They asked

Sava to name a candidate for the position of Serbian Archbishop and Sava told them to select one of his companions
from Hilandar, as each one of them was worthy of such a high
rank and responsible duty. Then the emperor said: "These, my
fathers and your brothers, are all venerable and saintly men,
but my soul wants you, because of your life from your youth is
known to us." Sava tried to convince his illustrious hosts of his
inadequacy and unworthiness for such a post, but in vain. His
reverend companions strongly supported the emperor. And the
patriarch insisted vehemently, saying to Sava: "Your people
need you, because you have wisdom coupled with authority. It
will be easier for you than for anyone else, with God's help.
And think it over, what merit it is to save only oneself by
solitude in the desert while a whole people are expecting salvation?" Sava resisted so that he made even the emperor angry.
Finally, he gave in and said, "God's will be done through you
upon me, a sinner."

And so Archimandrite Sava Nemanjić was consecrated Archbishop of Serbia by the Ecumenical Patriarch Manuel,
assisted by the Greek bishops and many Greek and Serbian
priests and deacons, in the presence of Emperor Theodore and
his civil and military dignitaries. This memorable event occurred in 1219, 894 years after the First Ecumenical Council in
Nicaea. On that day the Serbian Church received its first
spiritual leader.

After Sava's consecration, the emperor arranged great feasts
in his guest's honor, and rejoiced so much that his own people
wondered over his exultant joy. Moreover he gave rich gifts to
the patriarch, bishops and priests who took part in Sava's consecration, so much was he attracted by the personality of Sava.

Then the new Serbian Archbishop surprised the emperor and
the patriarch with a new petition. He asked that in the future
the Serbian Archbishops should be elected and consecrated by
the Serbian bishops. As the reasons for this new petition, he
pointed out the great distance between Serbia and Asia, in-

secure travelling conditions and the generally troubled world of those days. Both the emperor and the patriarch at first vigorously opposed the proposal, but after listening to Sava's arguments and realizing that he was worried about the unity and strength of the whole Orthodox Church, they finally agreed. The patriarch then wrote a "Grammata," a solemn official document, with the following text:

"I Manuel, the Ecumenical Patriarch, and the Archbishop of the city of Constantine, New Rome, in the name of our Lord Jesus Christ, have consecrated Sava Archbishop of all the Serbian lands, and have given him in God's name the authority to consecrate bishops, priests and deacons within his country; to bind and to loose the sins of men, and to teach all and baptize in the name of the Father, and of the Son, and of the Holy Spirit. Therefore, all ye Orthodox Christians, obey him as you have obeyed me."

When he received this "Grammata," Sava thanked the patriarch, and in prolonged talks asked many practical questions concerning the rule of the Church. The experienced patriarch answered all those questions gladly and wisely, and performed the Holy Eucharist several times with Archbishop Sava. Sava was asked to perform holy services without the patriarch in different churches of the city. The people were constantly seeking him to get his blessing, for this "barbarian" spoke better Greek than many Greeks. He fascinated the learned and the unlearned alike by his deeply spiritual sermons, refined manners and charity. While celebrating Liturgies or walking in the streets, he thought of the great saints of the Nicene Council, Sts Nicholas, Athanasius, Alexander, Spiridon, Eusebius, Achilles, James of Nisibis, Paphnutius and others, who in those historic days had celebrated in that same city and in the presence of Constantine the Great. With heartfelt thanks to the Lord he repeated the vow to adhere faithfully to the Creed those Fathers composed by the inspiration of the Holy Spirit there in Nicaea, where he now was moving, followed by a loving crowd of Christians.

Finally, Sava took leave of the emperor, and with the blessing of the patriarch he moved on. They both looked at the
vigorous Archbishop of Serbia with admiration and love. Did
Sava then foresee, looking with gratitude at his kind hosts, that
on his next visit to Nicea he would see another emperor and
another patriarch? Indeed this world is a place of meeting and
separation.

CHAPTER 25

SPIRITUAL POWER UNITED WITH AUTHORITY

A striking characteristic of a spiritual man is his dissatisfaction with himself. When elevated to a high ecclesiastical rank against his own will, he considers himself as having been belittled, almost punished. The Holy Mountain in the course of time has given to each Orthodox church very eminent bishops or archbishops, even patriarchs. None of them left the Holy Mountain willingly, including Sava.

Emperor Theodore and Patriarch Manuel showed great wisdom and sincere care for the welfare of the Serbian Church by insisting that Sava be her Archbishop. The Mother Church of Constantinople did not always show such a motherly disposition for sacrificing the privilege of her direct jurisdiction over a great church province. The emperor and the patriarch in Nicaea, however, did it readily and sympathetically as if moved by God's Spirit. They realized correctly that for a gigantic work ahead a giant was needed. But Sava, on the other hand, was absolutely sincere in refusing it. It was for him a vexing thought to be forever separated from the Holy Mountain, where he had for decades prepared and adorned his soul with all virtue so that it might be a worthy bride for the heavenly Bridegroom. Yet he could not continue this road to spiritual perfection. Therefore, returning from Asia Minor to the Holy Mountain by ship, his soul was clouded with sadness.

Here Sava was met with jubilation. Hilandar became overcrowded with monks from all the monasteries, kellia and caves "all eager to be blessed by him and sad to take leave of him." Nowhere in the world is a bishop so much respected and honored as on the Holy Mountain. The Protos himself and all the abbots invited Sava to celebrate the Liturgy, and to ordain new priests and deacons. They greeted him everywhere as their old friend and benefactor. Many of them still remembered him as a boy walking barefoot and helping everyone everywhere. And all of them knew him as a most rigorous ascetic, a most practical superior and a most charitable brother, so that they were now proud of him indeed. They were proud that the secular world with all its glory and vanity needed the monks of the Holy Mountain, respected their spiritual feats and appreciated their character. With his blue eyes swimming, Sava looked in deep love at each of those who had martyred themselves for God's love, always ready to weep for joy in their joy or for sadness in their sadness. After he had accomplished all he had been asked to do, he withdrew to his House of Silence.

There in his familiar dark cell, an overwhelming weakness suddenly gripped him. That cell, in which he had built a ladder to heaven for his soul, and in which he enriched himself so much with self-knowledge and with treasures of divine wisdom, now proved to be his Gethsemane. He felt as Adam did being driven from Paradise. In his agony he even protested to God crying: "O, my Lord, I have hoped in Thee, and now Thou hast let me fall very low by separating me from the saints of the Holy Mountain. I am not able to do any good for the people of my country."

But the Lord did not abandon His faithful servant. One night Sava was roused from a light sleep when the Holy Virgin appeared before him and said: "Why should you so despair since you know that I am interceding for you before the King of all, who is my Son and God? Get up therefore and go to the work for which He has selected you. Cast away all doubts because He will help you always."

Fortified by this vision, Sava got up, swiftly arranged all the affairs in Hilandar, took with him some of the ablest monks worthy of being bishops, and went on to Thessalonika. In this great city he stayed for a long time, taking for his residence the Monastery of Philokalos. With his disciples he set to work. He copied the indispensable canonical books, as well as liturgical ones. He bought a great number of Greek books to be later translated into Serbian, and a great quantity of church vestments, ikons and liturgical vessels. Whatever excellent object he saw in the churches of Thessalonika he ordered the artists to make for Zica and other monasteries in Serbia. Finally, he went to pray at the tomb of the Great Martyr Demetrios, took leave of the Metropolitan of Thessalonika, and moved on to Serbia.

At the Serbian frontier he was met by his nephews, Radoslav and Vladislav, the sons of his brother Stefan. The Grand Župan was unable to come because he was sick and in bed. The young princes greeted their uncle with exceeding joy and reverence, bowed before him, kissed his hands, and asked for his blessing.

So over six hundred years after the Serbs began to accept the Christian faith, the first Serbian archbishop set foot on Serbian soil—and what an archbishop!

THE LIVING AND THE
DEAD IN ACTION

A true man of God is a welcome visitor wherever he appears. Sava was greeted as warmly in the royal courts, in Constantinople and later in Nicaea as he had been by the monks on the Holy Mountain. Now, his return to Serbia was indeed a nationwide triumph.

Informed at the frontier of his brother's illness, Sava hurried with great speed to Ras. He was followed by a long cavalcade of men on horses and a trail of pack animals loaded with goods he had purchased or had received for use in the church. At Ras he found Stefan gravely ill, more so than he had been told. The attendants thought the Grand Zupan was dying. Sava, bent over his brother, offered prayers to God, aloud and mentally, and sprinkled him with holy water. The sickness quickly disappeared and Stefan got up and sat at the table with the archbishop and other members of the family. The joy of Sava's return was now doubled by the joy of Stefan's miraculous recovery.

When the two brothers were alone, Sava related to Stefan all his adventures in Nicaea and elsewhere during the past two years of their separation. And Stefan, filled with joy and humility, bowed before Sava and greeted him with these words: "Welcome to you who are sent by God to teach us, the people of your motherland, and to establish among us the laws and customs appropriate to a Christian nation; and I vow to be obedient to you as a servant to his Lord." This solemn vow Stefan kept faithfully to the end of his life. But this pledge also marks the end of the past unpleasant relationship between the two brothers, which may have caused Sava to leave Serbia two years before.

Afterward Sava requested Stefan to summon a council of

state dignitaries to decide upon the new dioceses and bishoprics. The territory of Raška, where the Serbs lived, had been split into two dioceses under the jurisdiction of the Archbishop of Ohrida. Sava created nine more, each with a bishop's seat in a monastery: Ras, centered in the Monastery of Peter and Paul; Toplica at the Monastery of St Nicholas; Moravica at the Monastery of St Achilles; Dabar at the Monastery of St. Nicholas; Budimlje at the Monastery of St George of the Columns; Hvosno at the Monastery of the Theotokos at little Studenica; and Prizren at the Monastery of the Theotokos. Prevlaka, on the seashore near Kattaro, had its center at the Monastery of the Archangel, and Ston, between Dubrovnik and Split in Dalmatia, was ruled from the Monastery of the Theotokos. The archbishop's residence was to be in Žiča, in the Monastery of the Ascension.

Satisfied with what he had accomplished in accord with the state authorities, Sava promptly proceeded to Studenica. With great emotion he embraced the sepulcher of St Simeon, his father, gave blessings to the abbot and all the brothers and at once started regular church services, during the day and at night. He ordained many priests and the necessary number of deacons. He gave instructions every day to the new priests how to lead a blameless life according to the holy faith, how to exhort the people to be cleansed from the remnants of pagan habits and vices, and how to combat heresies. He taught them how to perform church services, the sacraments and other prescribed rites. After he saw them thoroughly confirmed in the knowledge of all these matters, he sent them to vacant or newly-founded parishes. He also appointed protopresbyters, deans, and rural deans for all the districts to attend to the spiritual needs of the people and parish priests to serve as examples of a Christian life.

Meanwhile, the oil flowed regularly from the tomb and the ikon of St Simeon, and even more when Sava held all night vigils with heartfelt prayers. This continuing miracle streng-

thened the faith of the people enormously and helped Sava's
work. Sava's biographer writes: "The living and the dead
seemed to have made an agreement to strengthen their people
spiritually and morally through astonishment and joy, that is
through the Apostolic tongue of the one and the the flowing oil
of the other." Sava's vital words on the true faith were confirmed by the marvel of the aromatic flow from the dead body
of St Simeon. Stefan was, in spirit and truth, one with both of
them, venerating the father and obeying the brother.

Thus, these three in unity were dramatically building up a
nation spiritually and physically.

CHAPTER 27

THE ARCHBISHOP IN ŽIČA

A thought expressed in stone or color leaves a greater impression upon the human soul than when expressed in spoken words. It is recorded that the christianization of Russia was due to the famous church of St Sophia in Constantinople, to its amazing architectural grandeur and internal beauty. Its founder, Emperor Justinian, a countryman of St Sava, may be therefore called the Apostle of Russia with no less honor than Saint Vladimir.

Sava knew of the great value of Christian art in the propagation of the faith. Before Sava, Nemanja had also known this. He had built the graceful Studenica, and before that St George of the Columns. There is a story that a Turkish Pasha came with his soldiers with the intention of destroying this church, but when he entered it and saw its imposing structure, the colorful frescos of angels and saints covering the walls and the harmonious cupola, he became so frightened that he shouted: "Let us get away quickly, for God Himself dwells here!"

The Muslims recognized the striking power of religious art, but the Bogomils did not. They detested it and shunned it. The Muslims built great mosques, competing with the Christian church buildings. They even transformed the most beautiful Christian churches into mosques, as they did with St Sophia and with many other churches in the Balkans, including Serbia.

When Sava came to Žiča as the archbishop, he found and saw it architecturally finished. A lofty tower soared to dominating height. The church had a long single nave, a large altar, and a very spacious vestibule supported by two rows of columns. There was one great cupola with two smaller ones; two chapels on the flanks of the nave, and a third quite small chapel in the tower, to which Sava would retire for worship in seclusion. The whole church was built of stone, plastered with mortar, painted red with golden stripes at all joints and seams, both vertical and horizontal. It was encompassed by rectangular walls thick and high, with many turrets and battlements, meant for defense against aggression. Within the walls and all around the great church and the little church of the Holy Apostles were built the cells for the monks with larger refectories and halls, as well as apartments for the archbishop, the king and the guests.

All this Stefan had accomplished according to Sava's plan and instructions, and now to Sava's great satisfaction. But the internal adornments of the church, such as the fresco-painting of cupolas and walls, the carved stone, metal and woodwork, as well as the general furnishing of the church—all were waiting for Sava. Sava had brought with him purposely a considerable number of artists from Asia Minor, Thessalonika and others who had fled from Constantinople. Some had worked for him on Hilandar, all of them were known as the best masters in Byzantine art of the time. Sava did not want to imitate the mixed style of Studenica, his father's foundation, but intended to show in Žiča the purest Byzantine style as the perfect expression of Orthodoxy.

Always "aglow with the spirit" (Rom 2:11), Sava urged the artists to hurry the work as much as possible, although being highly gifted himself with artistic talent he knew quite well that art is hostile to haste. He on his part, however, was hostile to the quick passage of time. He wished to fill the limited time with events unlimited in greatness and importance. He was anxious to complete the solemn consecration of the great church, the ordination of the new bishops, Sava's own installation in it as the first Serbian Archbishop, the meeting of the great National Assembly, or Sabor, and the proclamation and coronation of the first-crowned Serbian King. In view of this agenda, Sava was in a hurry to finish Žiča. And he succeeded in finishing virtually all of it. The rest of the work of lesser importance he postponed until after the greater events, for he wanted to finish all these celebrations between Easter and Pentecost in the year of our Lord 1220.

A large crowd of people attended the consecration of Žiča. And after the consecration, according to the rule, Sava celebrated the liturgy every day. At nine liturgies he ordained nine new Serbian bishops. Tirelessly, he preached at every liturgy. He congratulated the Serbian people and called them to thanksgiving for now having bishops of their own blood and tongue. On the other hand, he taught the new bishops in private how to become worthy to be called the successors of Christ and the great apostles, both in their personal lives and in the performance of their public duties. "Your life," said he, "ought to be disciplined in order that you may serve as examples of all virtues to those under your care. For be sure that you shall have to give an answer even for the very least sheep of your spiritual flock to Jesus Christ, the Supreme Chief of all the pastors, when He appears at the Last Judgment." After many similar instructions and warnings, he distributed to them books in the Serbian language that he had brought from the Holy Mount and Thessalonica, ordering them to have the books copied and multiplied for use in every monastery and every parish church under their jurisdiction. Then he blessed them and sent them out as new apostles, each one to his own diocese.

Sava dedicated Žiča to Christ the Pantocrator, whose enormous fresco image was painted in the great cupola and whose feast day has been fixed from ancient times on Ascension Day, that is the fortieth day after Easter. Therefore, the archbishop sent word to the Grand Župan to come to Žiča on that day with his generals, noblemen and officers of the state, great and small. He also sent invitations to the bishops and other clergy to come to Žiča.

They all obeyed and came in time. Myriads of human eyes beheld with wonderment and joy beyond description.

CHAPTER 28

THE SABOR IN ŽIČA

No beauty can be compared with the beauty of holiness. That is why the visionary exclaimed: "O worship the Lord in the beauty of holiness!" (Ps 29:2). For only the beauty of holiness cleanses and elevates the human soul. It arouses two noble feelings in the hearts of men—awe and joy.

Days before the Great Feast, as is usual among the Orthodox, masses of people flocked to Žiča in order to find a place beforehand, and to feed their souls with the beauty of holiness. The spacious churchyard, both banks of the Žiča rivulet, the monastery meadow down below, the orchards and glens, hillocks and plains, all as far as the eye could see were filled with people, buzzing like bees in a hive. Tents were pitched as shade and huts of branches were hastily improvised for rest and sleep. City folk and peasants came in their best national hand-embroidered dress. The people from different provinces were recognizable by their distinct dress. All souls were lifted toward God, all eyes were directed toward the new marvel of a monastery, peering to see Sava, and expecting the Grand Župan and his escorts.

The troopers arrived first at a gallop, heralding the coming of the Grand Župan. The multitude of people, like leaves driven by a wind, rushed forward to see and to greet him. And Stefan arrived escorted by princes, Župans, chiefs of staff and other dignitaries, all clothed in rich and colorful attire, girded with gold or silver belts, according to their rank, and all set with precious stones. A military honor guard appeared behind them with glittering arms: swords, spears, maces, helmets and shields.

So the two brothers met again, no longer in their father's church but in their own. They greeted each other with tears expressive of their mutual love.

Stefan took a quick glance at Žiča, and was dumbfounded by its majestic glory and holy beauty. It struck him as if the sun had fallen to the earth. He overheard people saying: "Heaven on earth!" And he rejoiced exceedingly because it was to be called his church, his foundation, at Sava's suggestion.

After they had rested and refreshed themselves, the chimes called for Great Vespers, for it was the eve of the day of the Ascension. Sava showed Stefan the chair made for the archbishop. The church was filled to capacity with the chiefs of state, the clergy and the people. After the singing of the troparion, "Thou hast ascended in glory, O Christ our God," Sava stood up and delivered the following address: "You all know well how I twice ran away from you into the desert. You know also that of the many created beauties in this world, none of them took precedence over my love for God. Nor did I believe that any earthly treasure could bring me the happiness which is to be derived from turning to God in prayer. For your sake however, my compatriots, I left my holy and sweet desert and came to seek nothing else but your souls. In order to save your souls, I despised my own. In doing so, I remembered some ancient saints, who in pitying their compatriots spoke to God: 'If thou wilt, forgive their sin, but if not, blot me out of thy book' (Exod 32:32), or: 'I could wish that I myself were accursed and cut off from Christ for the sake of my brethren, my kinsmen by race' (Rom 9:3). Even so I, desiring to bring about your salvation, abandoned my own. But if you will follow my instructions in order to establish God's law among you, then you and I may assure our salvation. I ask you, therefore, to listen carefully to every word I say to you of God for your own benefit. For behold how the Lord God has strengthened, multiplied and enlarged you by the intercession of His servant, St Simeon. Many of you have become governors and chiefs, generals, and princes, some of you even Župans and Great Župans. It is not appropriate, however, that the man who stands above you, by God's grace, in power and dignity, should be called by the same name as some of you. But just as I have been ordained and clothed with the power of an archbishop for your sake, even so the man who, under God, is ruling our people ought to be distinguished from other dignitaries by a royal crown, as king. This will serve, I believe, for your own honor and glory. When this be accomplished, then I shall continue to speak to you of the divine faith and of your eternal salvation.''

In response to Sava's words, the people joyfully shouted: "You are sent to us by God, and we will obey you in everything.'' In those days loudspeakers of course did not exist. But a whisper quickly spread through the night to the multitudes outside: "Tomorrow, we shall have a king!"

CHAPTER 29

STEFAN THE FIRST-CROWNED KING

There are days in the history of a nation which remain unparalleled and forever memorable because they are the turning points in the destiny of that nation. Such a day was the Ascension of our Lord, (Spasovdan), in the year 1220. On that day the first Serbian archbishop was installed and the first Serbian king crowned in Žiča. Both of these events had the same meaning: full independence of the Serbian people from foreign authority, ecclesiastical as well as secular. And both were the work of Saint Sava.

On that day, Sava celebrated the liturgy in the great church "with all the bishops, superiors and many priests." The bishops first took him and installed him in the archbishop's throne. Then after the Great Entrance the archbishop took the consecrated crown and put it on the head of Grand Župan Stefan. He also put the royal purple over his shoulders. And lastly he anointed him with the holy chrism and communicated him at the altar. Then he proclaimed him: 'Stefan, King of all the Serbian lands and the sea-coast." The people shouted enthusiastically: "Amen, Amen—Long life to King Stefan!"

After that the new king offered hospitality and entertainment to all those present. By Sava's order, the poorest were brought before the king to receive gifts in order that they too might rejoice with the people rejoicing all around.

"The right-believing King rejoiced with inexpressible joy," says the biographer. He rejoiced most of all on account of the majestic Žiča, which would immortalize his name before God and the Serbian people forever. He went to get a closer view of the church outside, and to look at every nook and corner, at every detail. Nowhere could a church like it be seen in the whole Balkans except in Constantinople. In the portico there were two fresco paintings, one of Stefan himself and the other of Prince Radoslav, his eldest son and successor. The portait of Stefan shows a fine looking man with black beard and a sumptuous royal crown with pearls and hanging tassels on its edges. Such a crown was worn later by all the Serbian kings and tsars. We do not see the queen in that picture, as we are accustomed to see in every church of royal foundation. Nemanja was painted in Studenica with his wife Anna, for example. The reason is probably that Stefan's second wife was Roman Catholic.

In the same portico on the wall was written King Stefan's bequest and decree. In short, this writing explained the motives and intentions of the king in founding Žiča and enumerated the endowments for sustaining it. Instructions in procedure followed.

Enraptured by the transcendent beauty of Žiča, the king was glad beyond words. Says the biographer: "He did not rejoice so much because of the royal crown or because of the brilliant, regal purple. The real cause of his joy was Žica and the multitude of people admiring it and worshiping in it."

Stefan was certainly a deeply religious man. On the whole, he was a great man in spite of some of the human mistakes he made now and then. He sincerely repented of his mistakes before his spiritual father, Sava, and received forgiveness. A historian says of him: "Nemanja's successor, his son Stefan, was a wise and talented man, well educated in the Byzantine spirit. He was a skilful diplomat and a prudent warior. Without doubt he was one of the most gifted men among the descendents of Nemanja."

On the following day, Sava delivered a great sermon from his archbishop's chair, with the king and his attendants present. Sava started as usual by elucidating the fundamental truths of the Christian faith. He addressed the audience with these words: "Brothers and friends, my children in God, let my words be heard with attention and with your love for your benefit.'' The first part of the sermon was deeply theological and the second pastoral. After he had expounded the Christian faith as clearly as could be done, he then spoke of heresies and wrong teachings which the devil had sown among Serbs like tares in the wheat. He called on any who had fallen into heresies to return to the right faith saying: "and we shall quickly cure him by this right faith in God." To this a loud response came from the audience: "We believe, archbishop, as you teach us." The archbishop then asked all of them to repeat after him three times the Orthodox Creed "I believe in one God" to the end. Then he asked them to repeat after him: "We accept all the Councils of the Fathers of the Church, and whatever they rejected we reject and whatever they cursed we curse too. We venerate the holy Cross upon which Christ our Life was crucified. We venerate the ikons of Christ and His holy Mother. We take Holy Communion under two species with the firm belief that we are taking the real body and the real blood of our Savior. We venerate also the churches and the ikons of the saints. We shall adhere to the tradition of the Holy Apostles and other saints."

It was a striking scene, which could be compared with the scene on Jordan when John the Baptist shouted to the people: "Repent!" And all those who belonged to heresies sincerely repented and asked Sava what he wanted them to do.

King Stefan was very much moved. He always thought of his younger brother as being an extraordinary man, but he had hardly expected Sava to make such a profound transformation.

CHAPTER 30

THE END OF THE SABOR IN ŽIČA

In those days, in Orthodox countries, the problem of relations between the church and the state did not disquiet the people as it does in our days. These two forces balanced themselves, through long tradition. Whenever emperor tried to prevail over patriarch, or patriarch over emperor, each had to give way eventually. There existed no tradition in the Church of the East of an august priest, the Pontifex Maximus. There were unfortunate clashes between civil and ecclesiastic authorities on personal grounds, but those clashes were temporary and passing. If such clashes and disagreements arose on matters of religious doctrines and principles, threatening the unity of the Christian people, the Councils had to settle the issue. Whoever was found guilty could not escape condemnation by the Councils, be he emperor or patriarch or anybody else.

Sava's conception of mutual relations between church and state was founded upon a deeper conception of the aim of man's life on earth. He clearly realized that all rightful terrestrial aims should be considered only as a means toward a celestial end. He was tireless in pointing out the true aim of man's existence in this short life span on earth. That aim is the Kingdom of Heaven according to Christ's revelation. Consequently, both the church and the state authorities are duty-bound to help people toward that supreme end. If they want to compete with one another, let them compete in serving people in the fear of God and not by quarreling about honors and rights or usurping prerogatives from one another. The king and the archbishop are called to be servants of God by serving the people toward the final and eternal aim. "Seek first the Kingdom of God and His righteousness" (Mt 6:33)— that was

Sava's program for the Serbian national church and the state. This was the command not only to the apostles but to the laymen as well, and not only to archbishops, but to kings and other rulers. Ever since Sava, the tradition has been established "to choose the Kingdom of Heaven rather than an earthly kingdom." About 200 years later, the Serbian King Lazar led his devoted army with this watchword to the Battle of Kossovo against Muslim aggression. And with this watchword, thousands of Serbian martyrs have gone to their death. This watchword has been heard from the lips of priests, kings and martyrs alike until our day.

On the third day of the Sabor, Sava accomplished another important achievement. On Saturday, the eve of the Sunday dedicated to the Fathers of the First Ecumenical Council, who composed our Creed and condemned the evil heresy of Arius, Sava preached on the right faith and the importance of baptism. He must have thought of those who belonged to the Bogomil sect or to the Roman Church. He concluded with this warning to all who were present: "Neither can our striving to live a good life without the right faith in God be of any avail to us, nor can the right faith without good works make us worthy of seeing the face of the Lord. Let, therefore, both go together in order to make us perfect without any blemish. Faith can save us only if united with and expressed in good works, inspired by the love of God." So Sava defined the relation between faith and good works, a problem which would tear Western Christendom apart for centuries.

After Great Vespers was at an end, Sava asked only those of the Bogomils and Roman Catholics who wanted to be taken back into the Orthodox Church to remain in the church. The archbishop gave them clear instructions on what they should do. He first asked the Bogomils to condemn their heresy and then to undergo preparations for holy Baptism. From the Roman Catholics, who had already been baptized, he demanded first a condemnation of their heresy and then a loud recital of the ancient Creed of the First and Second Ecumenical Councils (without "Filioque"), after which they were to be anointed with chrism. In this way they were again incorporated into the Orthodox Church of their fathers. Sava also instructed all the bishops to use this same procedure with the converts from both heresies in their own dioceses, just as they had seen him doing in Žiča.

On the next day, that is Sunday, after the Thanksgiving Service in the great church, the Council in Žiča was concluded. The king with his company took leave and with blessings from the archbishop went away, hailed by the people's acclamations: "Long life to King Stefan!" Sava, however, instead of taking a much needed and well deserved rest, went up into the little chapel in the tower to continue giving thanks to God for all that had been done. Removing his brilliant archbishop's vestments, which he liked only in order to show the splendor of Christ the High Priest, and dressing in the coarse garb of a simple monk, he prostrated himself before the Lord. This was his true environment, his inspiration, his life. And while Serbian knights and the masses of people heading homeward spread his fame as the greatest among them, Sava in deepest humility before His Eternal Majesty said of himself: "I am a worm and not a man."

CHAPTER 31

THE STORM ALL AROUND

It has been customary among the Orthodox people in the Balkans from ancient times that when a poor man starts building his house, all the neighbors pitch in to help him with the work, with money or with material and when the house is completed, they rejoice in the joy of their neighbor. Unfortunately one can also find in our history wealthy Christian rulers who rejoiced in destroying what his neighbor, "his brother in Christ," had built.

The events in Zica, by which a stable foundation had been laid for an independent home of the Serbian people and for their normal spiritual and national well-being, excited a storm of envy and anger abroad. The most vehement protests came from the Hungarian King Andreas II, and the Archbishop of Ohrida, Demetrios Homatijan. Assen II, the Bulgarian, the son-in-law of Andreas, did not stir for the moment, although he resented it greatly. The Latin King of Constantinople although furious about the new kingdom, was at that time utterly unable to do anything about it. Pope Callistus II at once retaliated with a letter to the Archbishop of Bar, entrusting to this prelate full authority over all churches and monasteries on the seacoast, in Serbia, Bosnia and Travunia, not only the Latin but the Orthodox as well—"tam Latinorum quam Graecorum sive Slavorum." Theodore Angelos, however, the mighty Prince of Epiros and Albania, received the news of what happened in Žiča seemingly without much concern, because he was then busy with preparations for a personal campaign in other directions, and therefore did not want to spoil his friendly relationship with Stefan. Also his brother Manuel was married to a Serbian princess, Comnyna. Yet personally he sympathized with Homatijan, for he planned soon to be

101

crowned emperor by him.

King Andreas of Hungary was titular King of Serbia, an empty title given to the Kings of Hungary by the Pope. He did not want to sacrifice this title nor permit anybody else to have it. A short time before that he had returned from a crusade in Palestine without glory. To be deprived now of that title would be another blow to his pride. Therefore, he not only protested with abusive words, but he even declared war on the new King of Serbia. Stefan did his utmost to avoid war, but in vain. Then he asked Sava to go to try to pacify the Hungarian. Sava obeyed and went at once. According to tradition, he met King Andreas in Bachka, in the village of Kovilj. Sava was received by King Andreas with honor. And there, as with Strez, he began to talk evangelically, reminding the king of Christ's teaching: "Whatever ye would that men should do to you, do ye even so to them." But in the course of their conversation, Andreas became angry and used slanderous words against Stefan. Sava prayed silently to calm the storm. And, indeed, God helped him as He had helped the prophet Samuel (I Sam 12:16-18). This is how it happened.

Sava was staying at some distance from the Hungarian military camp under a tent with his traveling companions. The summer heat was scorching. The king sent food and wine every day from his headquarters to the Serbs. One day, Sava sent some of his men to ask the king for some ice because of the great heat, but the king could find no ice. Then Sava prayed to God for ice, and, in answer to his prayer, God let hail fall in great quantities, which covered the earth around the Serbian tent. Sava filled a plate with hail and sent it to the king with a note: "I asked for ice from you, O King, and you could not get it; therefore I asked it from our Creator, who possesses all riches and all power. And behold, He gave it to me, and now I am sending it to you."

In great consternation King Andreas changed his mind, came hurriedly to the Serbian tent, bowed before Sava and called him "my spiritual father," asking forgiveness for his rude words. For several days the king sat at Sava's feet and listened to his spiritual teachings. Finally he expressed his wish to become Orthodox, and Sava fulfilled his desire. At their parting, King Andreas presented Sava with many gifts, some for himself and others for King Stefan, saying, "Give Stefan, the King of the Serbs, your brother and mine, my greetings and sincere love." Also he gave Sava an honor guard to escort him to the border at the great river Danube. Thus God helped Sava calm the storm threatening Serbia from the north.

The storm from the south was stirred up by Homatijan, the Archbishop of Ohrida. He directed an epistle to "monk" Sava through Jovan, Bishop of Skoplje. In this epistle, he accused Sava of having transgressed the canonical laws of the Church and of violating his monastic vows and moral discipline. Homatijan charged that it was uncanonical for Sava to go to Nicaea instead of to Ohrida to ask for the independence of the Serbian Church; it was uncanonical for him to become archbishop without first being a bishop; his interventions with foreign princes and kings concerning military and diplomatic affairs were also uncanonical. Sava should not have abandoned his hermit life on the Holy Mountain and become a prince of the church; it was unethical for him to live amidst the temptations of worldly society, riding good horses, banqueting in luxury in the company of noblemen, and leading a life of luxury. Besides this letter of criticism to Sava, Homatijan sent protests twice to the Ecumenical Patriarchs of Nicaea, first to Manuel in 1220 and second to Germanos in 1222.

The patriarchs passed over all these accusations, serious though they seemed to be, in silence, for they recognized their futility. Sava went to Nicaea and not to Ohrida because the Archbishop of Ohrida himself was under the supreme authority of the Patriarch of Constantinople, who then resided in exile in Nicaea. Sava was made archbishop from a monk, as is usual in the Eastern Church. Even some laymen had been elevated to the offices of archbishop and patriarch (Ambrose, Nectarius, Photius). Also, many patriarchs and popes, both before and after Sava, had intervened with the foreign rulers in order to avert wars and slaughters among their Christian people. Of necessity the archbishop had to move among all kinds of people as even the apostles had done, but still he led a most rigid ascetic life. Besides, Sava's character and his saintly life were at that time well known from Hungary to Nicaea. Therefore, Homatijan's accusations of Sava were disregarded.

So the storm was calmed, the danger passed, and Sava continued his constructive work. Thanks to him, the Serbian Church and the Serbian Kingdom now stood firm and secure, under the sole protection of Christ the Pantocrator.

CHAPTER 32

THE LAST DAYS OF
KING STEFAN

The intelligence of a Christian may be measured by his awareness of approaching death and his preparations for a life to come. For "it is appointed unto men to die once, and after that comes judgment" (Heb 9:27), so logically we should make preparations while we still are on this side of death. Truly, we are not lulled by false doctrines of reincarnation, that is to say, of many deaths and many lives; but we are awakened to the stern reality of only one life and one death on earth "and after that judgment." This is the direct teaching of Christ (Lk 16:19-31). Due to this teaching, the followers of Christ are inspired to deeds unparalleled in the history of mankind.This life-span of ours on earth is our only chance. The heathen philosophers used to say: "Let us enjoy today, for tomorrow we die." A Christian, however, says: "Let us work today, for tomorrow we are judged!"

The two brothers, Sava and Stefan, indeed filled their days with good works in watchful expectation of death. Stefan followed the example of his father and even more that of his brother. His admiration of Sava kept increasing as he saw his spiritual achievements, his indefatigable activity, his intrepidity in the face of death and his agonizing efforts in preparation for the world beyond. The older he grew the more fervently Stefan followed the pattern of his brother monk. After his coronation in Žiča and the calming of the storms caused by it, he, "the right believing King, had peace on all sides, and lived happily glorifying God." As he had been courageous in war, so he was in peace an ever busy student, a warm-hearted friend and benefactor, an excellent writer, a charming conversationalist, a God-fearing and modest man. In all his happiness and peace, however, he thought of the termination of life and of the

judgment, just as Sava did. He could not fail to remember and
to see the plaque the monks of Studenica used to put over the
doors of their cells with the inscription: "Remember the hour
of death and you never will sin." He liked monks not only
because Sava liked them but because of their constant remembrance of death and their preparations for another life in eter-
nity. Indeed, he himself wanted to become a monk. Why not?
Had not his father become a monk, and his brother Sava too?
And did his mother Anasasia not die as a nun? Even his elder
brother Prince Vukan took monastic vows, and died as the
monk Theodosius, and was buried in Studenica beside St Simeon. Sava, the first monk in their family, must have explained to them what monkhood meant. To those who take
monastic vows, many sins are forgiven, and new grace is
bestowed upon them by God to prepare themselves more
diligently for the future life.

King Stefan now was getting on in years. He was over sixty, a
widower, and often attacked by illness. He, therefore, asked
Sava to make him a monk. Sava postponed it. He repeated his
request, and Sava again postponed it. Once, while very ill, he
sent a messenger to get Sava. Sava arrived and with prayers
made him whole, but did not make him a monk, although
Stefan said that he preferred to become a monk rather than live
any longer. We do not know Sava's reasons for refusing his
brother's wish. Probably by postponing it, he wanted to delay
a change in the royal throne as long as possible.

But in the fall of the same year, Sava received a mesage that
Stefan was dying. With great speed he rushed from Žiča on
horseback. Nearing the capital, he met a group of new
messengers who weepingly informed him that the king was
dead. They told him also that Stefan's last words were: "Sava,
Sava!" Before that, they said, the state dignitaries had
assembled around the king's death bed, and had asked him
which of his four sons should be his successor. The dying king
answered: "My kingdom is not mine, but my brother's—ask

Sava." Hearing this, Sava at once began to use all his spiritual means in his struggle against his brother's death. He prayed silently to the Lord to raise the king, not in order to live much longer but only in order to become a monk. "Command, O Lord, thy angel," prayed he, "to return the soul of thy servant, and my brother, to live only until the evening of this day, that I may install him into thine angelic monastic order as he desired." Upon coming to the chambers of his brother and seeing his dead body, Sava put his right hand into his bosom and with his fingers made the Sign of the Cross upon his heart in the name of the Holy Trinity. Then he said in a loud voice, "Get up, my lord, and speak!" Stefan opened his eyes, grasped Sava's hand and kissed it. Then he got up and spoke. After that, Sava took by the hand Radoslav, the eldest son of Stefan, and brought him to the king in order to proclaim him his successor. Then the king said: "I give him my regal scepter; give him your blessing." Sava then clothed Stefan with a monk's garb and changed his name. Instead of King Stefan, he became now the monk Simon.

In the evening, Stefan—or the monk Simon—leaning on the breast of Sava "sweetly gave up his ghost." Thus ended the earthly life of a great Christian king, a great saint, on September 24, 1228.

The body of the late king was brought in a great procession from Ras to Studenica and buried there near St Simeon. After that, Sava distributed alms to the poor for the repose of the soul of his beloved brother, the First-Crowned King, Stefan, who died as the monk Simon.

CHAPTER 33

THE FIRST PILGRIMAGE

Sava did not mourn much over his dead brother. He mourned only for his separation from such a noble and strong supporter of his plans for making the Serbs into a nation holy unto God.

After the proper burial of King Stefan, Sava invited the king's eldest son, Radoslav, to Žiča to be crowned. A new door was opened in the great church, through which the new king should enter. Radoslav came, entered the church through the new door, and was received there with love by his loving uncle. Sava instructed him to follow the examples of his grandfather and his father, took an oath from him to be a true Orthodox Christian in faith and in conduct, and crowned him with a royal crown in the presence of all the Serbian nobility and a great mass of people. After the coronation, King Radoslav went out through the same newly-opened door, and then the door was closed forever. So the king's oath was preserved in the church, never to be betrayed.

Then Sava made preparations for a pilgrimage to the Holy Land. This had been a long cherished desire of his. Now, after he had secured for Serbia a new lawful king and had seen peace and order established, it was an appropriate time for him to carry out his pious desire. King Radoslav with all his dignitaries and bishops implored him not to leave them. They feared that Sava would not come back again, which was an intolerable thought to them. But Sava cheered them, blessed them, and rode down to the Adriatic seacoast, where his nephew Great Župan George, the son of Vukan, ruled. Having blessed the people, Sava boarded the ship and turned his face towards Jerusalem.

It happened at that same time that the Sixth Crusade had

been undertaken by a great German Emperor, Frederick II, the grandson of Frederick Barbarossa, a friend of Nemanja. This Frederick II was a dauntless warrior and a skillful diplomat. He was "alone of all Crusaders who was not blessed, but cursed by the Pope." But he alone succeeded in securing freedom for Jerusalem and the Holy Land for a full fifteen years by a treaty with the Arabian sultan, without shedding a drop of human blood. This was the only bloodless crusade.

Thus Sava had no trouble getting to Jerusalem and traveling in the Holy Land. In Jerusalem he was received by Patriarch Athanasius with brotherly affection. The patriarch offered to Sava and his companions hospitality in his own residence as long as they stayed in the Holy City. Sava celebrated the Holy Eucharist, sometimes with the patriarch and at other times alone, in the Church of the Resurrection. He went up to Zion where the Lord had held His Last Supper and had washed the feet of His disciples. He walked down to Gethsemane, where Jesus in agony prayed to His heavenly Father. And there in the same grove of olive trees, Sava, full of sorrow, falling on his face, glorified the sorrowing Savior of the world. He followed as it were his betrayed and bound Lord to the house of Caiaphas, where the Righteous One was judged by the enemies of righteousness, who buffeted, and beat Him and spat in His face. He followed Him to the Praetorium, where Governor Pilate pronounced Him innocent and yet permitted Him to be mocked and whipped by Roman soldiers, and finally crucified. Sava ascended the Via Dolorosa up to Golgotha. There, prostrated before the Crucifix, he moistened the ground with warm tears. Then he stepped down and entered the sepulcher where he contemplated the dead body of Christ in the tomb and His soul in Hades. He contemplated also His glorious Resurrection, the glittering whiteness of angels and the tremulous joy of the women, the myrrhbearers. After that, he climbed up the Mount of Olives to the spot from which the risen Lord ascended to heaven, escorted by holy angels, as

witnessed by His disciples. In his spirit, Sava saw the whole
scene very vividly and heard the great prophecy of the angels:
"This Jesus, who was taken up from you into heaven, will
come the same way as you saw Him go into heaven." (Acts
1:11). Visualizing Christ ascending to heaven as the crowning
event of His divine mission on earth, Sava felt great satisfaction in having dedicated Žiča to the Ascension of the Lord. So
with his whole vibrant soul, Sava had gone through the deepest
pit of Christ's painful suffering and humiliation to the very
zenith of His triumph. And finally, filled with joy, he had
returned from the place of the Ascension to the altar of the
Resurrection.

But without losing himself in mere contemplations and vision, our Saint also showed here his usual practical sense. He
was searching for any occasion to do some charitable or useful
deed in the name of his Lord. On two such occasions these were
presented to him by Providence, one in Acre and the other in
Jerusalem. During previous crusades, the Latins had taken by
force St George's Orthodox Church in Acre, which belonged to
the Monastery of St Sava the Sanctified and which had been used for centuries as a hostel for pilgrims. Sava at once bought
that church from the Latins and returned it to its rightful pro-
prietors. And because our Sava showed such goodness to the
monastery founded by his namesake of old, the monks of that
monastery ever since have received Serbian pilgrims there with
brotherly love. The second instance was this: the Muslims held
in their possession the House with the Upper Room where our
Lord had celebrated His Last Passover with the disciples. Sava
was shocked and saddened by the fact that one of the most
sacred Christian places should be in the hands of the infidels.
Taking council with the patriarch, Sava promptly bought that
place for a great sum of gold and made it the possession of the
Serbian Orthodox Church.

After tarrying for a fairly long time in the Holy City, Sava
asked from the patriarch his permission and blessing to pro-

ceed to visit churches, monasteries and other holy places in Palestine. The patriarch gladly gave him a letter of recommendation and bid him farewell. With this document in his hands, our saint quickly left the walls of Jerusalem behind.

CHAPTER 34

IN HIS MASTER'S STEPS

If you make a pilgrimage to Palestine expecting to see beautiful landscapes, you will be disappointed. Much more beautiful landscapes may be seen in America, Switzerland or in the Balkans. There is nothing very striking, nothing extraordinary over there. And yet it is the most attractive land on the globe because of Him who is called "fairest of all the sons of men" (Ps 45:2). The personality of Christ makes this land exceptionally beautiful and attractive.

In Sava's time the Holy Land was the picture of ruin and desolation. Five crusades had trampled over it. Indeed one is at a loss to say who has made the deepest scars on its face or who did more to desecrate it, the votaries of the Crescent or those of the Cross. Sava neither dwelt upon the beauty of Serbia, his motherland, nor cared to tarry for long among the sad desolation of his Savior's motherland. He looked only upon the Savior, eager to worship Him at every step where there was a reminder of Him.

In Bethlehem, Sava stepped down to the rocky cave in which Jesus was born of the Holy Virgin. In Nazareth, he visited Joseph's house where the Archangel Gabriel announced to Mary that she was chosen by God to give birth to the King of Kings. He climbed Mount Tabor where Christ had revealed His divinity at His Transfiguration. He went to Cana, where at a marriage feast He had changed water into wine, "the beginning of his miracles." From there he proceeded to the Sea of Galilee, upon and around which the Lord had expounded His new doctrines and performed awesome miracles. He traveled down the Jordan River to where John the Baptist had baptized Jesus. He crossed the river to see the lifeless desert where John had lived for thirty years, and where later on a Serbian girl,

Sveta Petka, for the same length of time had emulated "the lion of the desert." He visited the Monasteries of St John and St Gerasim, after which he went through Jericho to the Mount of Temptation where Jesus after His baptism, was tempted by Satan. There in a Greek monastery, the altar is built upon the very rock upon which Jesus, according to tradition, had stood fasting for forty days and forty nights during His temptation. On that altar Sava celebrated the Holy Eucharist. Then he visited caves around the Dead Sea to see and talk with Christian hermits. Being always fond of hermits, he was eager to learn from them. He gave them liberal gifts, urging them to pray for him, for the departed King Stefan, and for all the living and dead among his spiritual flock. Then on the road from Jericho to Jerusalem, he visited the great lavra of St Euthemius and St Theoctistus, the Monastery of Choziball and that of St Chariton, everywhere eager to learn something useful, and ready to help with charity. In Bethany, he visited the home of Lazarus, on whom the Lord had performed the greatest of all miracles, raising him from the dead four days after after he had died and had been buried. Finally, he stopped for a longer stay at the famous Monastery of St Sava the Sanctified, Mar Saba. In this monastery our saint was received most cordially, and for good reason, as we have said before, and also because of an ancient prophecy which was still kept alive there among the monks. When Mar Saba, the founder of that monastery, was near his end, he told the monastic brothers that in the distant future there would come to their monastery a great archbishop, a man of God, his namesake, from a far-off western country. He bequeathed his staff, called Paterica, and two precious ikons of the Holy Virgin, to be given to that man of God whenever he should come. Now the monks recognized in the person of the Serbian archbishop that man of whom St Sava the Sanctified prophetically spoke. And they presented to him the staff and the two ikons.*

* The ikons were the Mother of God OF THE THREE HANDS (28 June & 12 July) and THE MILK-GIVER (12 January).

Patriarch Athanasius most enthusiastically received information about Sava from all those places which he had visited, news of his inspired church services, of his wisdom and his charity. Therefore on Sava's return to Jerusalem, Athanasius received him with an embrace and with gratitude. With the increasing fame of Sava, the name of Serbia and the Serbians became known in the Holy Land.

Thereupon, Sava prepared for his departure. He asked the patriarch to remember him and his people in the prayers at the Holy Sepulcher, exchanged gifts with him and started off. In Acre he stayed at St George's until he found a ship sailing to Asia Minor, for he wanted again to visit the emperor and the patriarch in Nicaea.

Theodore Laskaris and Patriarch Manuel were no more among the living. The new emperor was Theodore's son-in-law, John Vatatzes (1222-1254) and the new patriarch, Germanos. Both of them remembered Sava from his first visit to Nicaea to their predecessors. Later they had heard very much of him from the West and from the East. They received Sava as an old friend and as a holy man, and for many days they enjoyed his stories of the Holy Land. Sava celebrated liturgies with the patriarch and the Greek clergy in the historic churches of Nicaea, the masses of people pressing upon him to be blessed. The people of Nicaea remembered well how Sava had blessed them as a new archbishop. The emperor and the empress also asked him as a saintly man to bless them and remember them in his prayers. The empress recounted what a high opinion of Sava her father, the late Theodore, had had. Sava for his part spoke of the necessity of unity of all Orthodox nations, and of the reconciliation of the Greeks with the Bulgarians. The emperor and the patriarch complained about the Prince of Epiros who wanted to be Emperor of Byzantium; of Homatijan, the Archbishop of Ohrida, who wanted to be patriarch himself; and of the King of Bulgaria who officially recognized the Pope. At the end the emperor and empress handed Sava "much gold" saying: "We know your habit of giving charity to the needy; take this therefore, use it as you like, and pray for us sinners." And in order to honor him more, the emperor ordered one of his ships to take the Serbian archbishop to Mount Athos. He also ordered a captain with armed men to accompany him, for in those days the sea was swarming with pirates.

After arriving safely at the Holy Mountain, Sava was received enthusiastically as usual by the Protos and many others down to the last hermit, this time not only as an archbishop from among themselves, but as a pilgrim also. Sava wrote a letter of gratitude to Emperor John and to the patriarch, and sent home the captain and his soldiers with gifts. The gold he had received in Nicaea he quickly distributed, as from the emperor's own hand, to the poor monasteries and the hermits, adding to it some of his own.

After this Sava went to his House of Silence. There in solitude he contemplated all his experiences and impressions from his pilgrimage, offering hearty thanks to God for everything. In Hilandar he found all in order. He praised the abbot and the brothers, and gave them some new instructions based on his experiences in the East. He was never too tired to remind the monks of the Kingdom of Heaven as the ultimate goal of their toils and exercises. Finally, embracing and blessing them all, he left Hilandar and the Holy Mountain, never to see them again in his earthly life. He left, however, the Ikon of the Holy Virgin OF THE THREE HANDS, which he brought from Mar Saba of Jerusalem, to be regarded as the "abbess" of Hilandar.

In Thessalonika, he found a new ruler, Orthodox instead of Latin. He was Theodore Angelos, the former Prince of Epiros, the father-in-law of King Radoslav. After conquering Thessalonica, Adrianople and Thrace from the Latins, he had been crowned in that city as emperor by Archbishop Homatijan, Sava's adversary. Now Theodore needed Homatijan no more, so he therefore received the Serbian archbishop "with great hospitality, honors and gifts." Together with the Metropolitan of Thessalonika, he urged Sava to influence King Radoslav "to live with them in love and peace," which certainly Sava, as a peacemaker, could have easily promised to do. On his part Sava warned the ambitious emperor to abstain from hostility toward the King of Bulgaria and the Emperor of Nicaea. It was a wise and prophetic warning which, unfortunately, Theodore did not heed, to his own destruction.

Again Sava stayed in his monastery of Philokalos, where he celebrated liturgies in St Demetrius church and in other famous churches of Thessalonika. And then, escorted by a guard of honor which the emperor gave him, he left for Serbia, where he was greatly needed.

King Radoslav met his uncle with great joy and filial love.

CHAPTER 35

SHEPHERD AND LEADER

Innumerable saints remain unknown to men and are known to God alone. Christ's heavenly Kingdom would be pitifully small if it consisted only of those saints whose names are recorded in our calendar. God does not reveal to the world all His saints, only a very few according to the religious need of a time or of a nation. Through the miracles of those few revealed saints, God seeks to revive, strengthen or justify the faith of men of different countries or places. The history of the Serbian Church is proof of this.

Returning home from his pilgrimage, Sava at once proceeded to Studenica. He hastened to be in time for the annual memorial for his brother King Stefan. After the service, the tomb of the late king-monk was opened and the body found whole and undecayed. From it came a pleasant fragrance. All the people rejoiced, understanding it to be God's new blessing upon their country. The Almighty had enriched it with a new saint.

Sava knew at once what to do. Without delay he transferred the body of the new saint with all due honors to Žiča, for this was King Stefan's church and Sava therefore thought it was proper and fitting that his body should rest there. So King Stefan, who became a monk before his death with the name Simon, became after death St Simon. The people, however, until our day have called him Saint King, Sveti Kralj.

In this event Sava saw a new proof of God's grace and mercy. More encouraged than ever, he went out again on the great mission of preaching the gospel, healing the moral wounds of sinners and uniting all the people by faith and love into one sanctified body before God. In the monasteries he described to the monks various monastic rules from Asia and Palestine,

117

advising them to accept those which would be best for them and applicable to their country. His idea from the beginning was to make of the monasteries not merely places for working out the personal salvation of a number of monks, but also examples of working holy communities for the masses of people. Those in power he warned not to be overbearing and arrogant, but to fear God, to be "meek and charitable, forbidding anyone to be tormented by violence." He also warned the rich not to rely too much upon transitory riches but to "enrich themselves with good deeds," especially with charity toward the poor and weak. "You are made of the same earthly dust as they, and you depend on God as they on you," said Sava. He taught them to be of strong faith, rich in love, and not to return evil for evil, but to share their bread and clothing with the destitute without despising any man, however insignificant he might be. He especially stressed two virtues: charity and chastity. The evil of lust was rampant in those days everywhere in Europe, even among the new Slavonic nations in the Balkans. Sava spoke vehemently against those who defiled their bodies by fornification or adultery and other perverse habits. Often with tears he implored such sinners to rid themselves of their impure practices, which only make the devil rejoice. "For God has not called us for uncleanness but holiness" (I Thess 4:7). Persistently, he urged all Serbs, male and female, to keep lawful marriage in honor and to rejoice in legitimate children.

Sava's noble ambition was to make of the Serbs a holy nation, according to the Lord's saying: "You shall be holy as I am holy" (Lev 19:2; I Pet 1:16). When the Lord God commanded Israel, a people who were supposed to be made holy through the blood of bullocks, how incomparably more does He expect a Christian people to be holy through the blood of His only Son? Probably Sava was requiring too much of a people still wavering between heathenism and Christianity on the one hand, and between Orthodoxy and heresies on the other. But the prophets and apostles were just as demanding. "Be ye as I am," wrote St. Paul, and in his epistles he called all Christians "saints." What Paul preached in the first century, Sava preached in the thirteenth. He also could say to his Serbs: "Be ye as I am," for he was a shining example in word and deed. Following Christ's instruction, "Do and teach" (Mt 5:19), he first acted righteously and then taught. Thus nobody could ever accuse him of hypocrisy, which is the plague of many teachers who are not doers.

The people obeyed their shepherd readily, repented and changed. For such are men: if you ask them to be a little better, they will remain as they are; but if you put before them perfect patterns and urge them to be very good, they will more readily obey. As usual, Sava had much more difficulty with the aristocracy. Yet the majority followed him gladly. And all of them, the just and the unjust, looked at him, their spiritual leader, "as a luminary radiating God's light."

CHAPTER 36

THE PRESERVER

The history of mankind offers many lessons to those who would learn. One lesson is that it is more difficult to preserve what has been gained than to win new battles. This is true not only of empires created by conquest, but also of a people of the same blood, religion and tongue when united in a single national state after a long period of strife and separation. Modern examples confirming this are Germany and Italy, and earlier instances are offered by Russia, Great Britain and even France. The difficulty in preserving national unity once achieved has always been caused by the centrifugal reaction of a haughty and selfish aristocracy. The masses of people, if not misguided, are by some intelligent instinct always centripetal.

With enormous difficulties, Nemanja had succeeded in virtually uniting the Serbian people into one state. But soon after his death, the national state he created would have been broken into pieces, had it not been for Archbishop Sava, its God-sent preserver. He had controlled Vukan, his eldest brother, to bring him to repentance and to make him a monk. Afterwards he taught and guided Grand Župan Stefan, both before and after he had crowned him a king, until the very end. Now instead of his brothers, Sava had to deal with his nephews, which was harder work.

Sava had seven nephews; three sons of Vukan, and four of Stefan's. Vukan's sons were George, Stefan and Dmitar. George had relinquished his title of "king," most probably at the insistence of his uncle Sava, and recognizing his uncle, Stefan, as the real king, had called himself Great Župan. All of the three brothers were devout, and had built churches, emulating their grandfather Nemanja. Two of them had become monks. George had restored several old churches in his region. Stefan had built the great monastery of Moraca in Montenegro, which still exists as a great national sanctuary. Dmitar also had built a church, which was called Davidovc, after his monastic name David.

King Stefan had four sons: Radoslav, Vladislav, Uros and Predislav. The first three were to rule successively as Kings of Serbia, whereas Predislav, inspired by his uncle, Sava, had taken monastic vows and later on had become Archbishop Sava II.

After the death of King Stefan, the sons of Vukan claimed no right to the Serbian royal throne, most probably due to the pacifying influence of Sava. Sava wanted to establish an order of royal succession in the line of Stefan, the first-crowned king, always giving priority to the eldest son of a deceased parent. Therefore he crowned Radoslav king in Žiča. This done, Sava left Serbia, as we have seen, and went on a pilgrimage to the Holy Land.

King Radoslav was a man of meek character and weak as a ruler. He was educated by his mother Eudokia, an imperial Greek princess, and he was married to the Greek princess, Anna Duken, daughter of the mightiest of the Balkan rulers, Theodore Angelos, whom we have mentioned before, the crowned Greek emperor. So King Radoslav, being under the Greek influence both of his mother and of his wife, was regarded by the Serbs as more a Greek than a Serb. His wedding ring had a Greek inscription. His official papers were in Greek, as well as his seal and signature. It was presumed that his father-in-law directed the foreign policy of Serbia. And what was worst of all, his secret correspondence with Homatijan of Ohrida, Sava's great adversary, came to light. All these suspicions excited dangerous dissatisfaction with Radoslav among the Serbian nobility. They hated his wife and they despised him.

Such a state of affairs faced Sava on his return from the East. Knowing his nephew intimately, his uncle liked him and tried his best to preserve the kingdom from threatening disruption. But soon there came a change in the balance of power in the Balkans. In 1230, the Bulgarian king, Asen, defeated Emperor Angelos at Kokotnica, took him prisoner and blinded him. As a result, his son-in-law Radoslav's position became untenable. He fled with his wife through Dubrovnik, which symphathized with him to Durrazzo in Albania, where he found shelter with the family of his wife. But there again bad luck followed him. His wife, like a new Delilah, fell in love with a French duke and shamelessly fled from her husband.

So the unfortunate King Radoslav, abandoned by all and protected by none, moneyless and friendless in a foreign land, in fear even for his life, did not know what to do. His father was dead, his brother Vladislav was his enemy, his father-in-law was now a blind prisoner in Bulgaria, and his wife was the wife of another. His only hope was in his holy uncle, Sava, so he decided to return to Serbia and ask for the protection of his only friend. Sava shielded him from danger and made him a monk under the name of John. By this act at least his life was saved.

His wife, the ex-queen Anna Duken, soon became disappointed in her new husband, abandoned him and retired to an Orthodox convent where she lived to the end of her life as a nun.

The political group which proclaimed Radoslav's younger brother Vladislav king, expected the archbishop's approval, however. They knew very well that Sava had the people with him, and that without Sava and the people the new king would not be secure in his throne. Sava was very angry with all this violent and unlawful procedure, yet he thought first of preserving the nation and the state as a whole from the worst. Having saved Radoslav's life, he did not oppose what could not be repaired. He wisely arranged for the marriage of Vladislav with Bjeloslava, daughter of Asen, the King of Bulgaria. Now a third door was opened in Žiča, for the third and last king whom Sava himself crowned, instructed, warned and blessed.

After all this, Sava, tired and disappointed, retired to his House of Silence in Studenica. He had a presentiment that it was for the last time. There in solitude he offered a strange prayer to God, to let him die in a foreign country. Why, we do not know. Perhaps, as a good psychologist, he might have thought his death away from Serbia would be the strongest protest against those who sowed disorder in his country. Or perhaps, he might have thought that his death in a foreign country would cleanse the conscience of the people more and make them more willing to keep his laws and teachings, like Licurgus in ancient Sparta. Or perhaps, hindered from doing all he wanted to do for his people within Serbia, he prayed to God to let him go and work for his people from the outside. Most probably, all these three reasons together contributed to his strange decision, for the enlightened mind of Sava always knew what was best for his people.

CHAPTER 37

ARSENIJE

A truly great man is concerned with choosing a successor who is worthy of him. He wishes his successor to be greater than himself. On the other hand, a short-sighted leader may agree with the foolish king who said, "After us the deluge!"

Sava had been observing the worthiest of his disciples to select his successor, who would be able to continue his work. Of course he prayed to God for light and guidance. One day an unknown young man came to Žiča. He told the attendant of the archbishop about his life and his desire. He was from Srem and had heard of the holy life of Sava, of Žiča, and of the great number of monks there. He had been impressed by the talk he had heard of the unearthly beauty of that monastery and the monastic life of purity, work, and constant glorification of the Lord. He wished to be received as the least in the brotherhood. The attendant ushered him to the archbishop. With his penetrating spirit, Sava recognized in this young man spiritual greatness, although undeveloped, and he liked him from the first. He accepted him as a novice. For years Sava observed this young man, and was glad to see him rapidly progressing in spiritual growth, in knowledge and painstaking observance of every monastic rule. He clothed him in monastic garb and gave him the name Arsenije. Later he ordained him a deacon, then a priest, and made him ecclesiarch, that is, the supervisor of the great church of Žiča and all church services. Up in the wall of the great church Sava had made a small balcony with a screen-ed window through which he used to observe unseen the behavior of the monks during worship. Arsenije proved to exceed all the others in reading, preaching and arduous praying. Sava used to put him to the test in the presence of other monks in order that all the others should be convinced of Arsenije's

124

excellence over them. Here is one instance: Sava knew that Arsenije lived on bread and water except on feast days. On one such feast day, when the brothers were supposed to get cooked food and a cup of wine, Sava managed to put before Arsenije a dish of watery stew and a cup of vinegar. Anyone else would have protested, but Arsenije, indifferent to food, ate and drank without protest. Then other monks marveled and his master rejoiced over it. Indeed, Sava rejoiced seeing that Arsenije was perfect in all virtues—a perfect monk and a perfect man. Yet he still was uncertain about his choice until the Lord Himself revealed to him that his choice was God's choice too. Then Sava called Aresenije and told him of his plan to go again to the Holy Land, and also of his intention to make him archbishop in his stead.

"O, my holy father," cried Arsenije, "let me alone. I am a sinner unworthy of such dignity. Or take me with you, for I cannot bear separation from you."

Hearing this, Sava confided to him, "God himself has revealed to me that you are chosen for this duty. Therefore, obey God's command."

After long resistance and tearful pleadings, Arsenije bowed saying, "Let the will of God and of Your Holiness be done."

Then Sava suggested to King Vladislav to call the Sabor in Žiča. And when it was assembled, Sava first confidentially told the king of his intention "to lay down the archbishop's office and to go and die in some foreign land." This was a terrible shock to the king, for he needed the wise, strong support of his uncle more than anyone else. He must have remembered the last words of his father, King Stefan: "My kingdom is not mine, but my brother Sava's." He was conscious of the troubles and pains he had inflicted upon Sava by his toleration of the conspiracy against Radoslav. Ashamed of himself and repentant, he implored the saint not to leave him. But his magnanimous uncle, without reproaching him, calmly review-ed all the sorrowful events and comforted the king by describing to him the strength of his position. What had been established and proclaimed in Žiča thirteen years ago was now firmly consolidated. The Serbian kingdom was recognized, the Hungarian king pacified and befriended, and the danger of the revolution because of a feud between the two brothers peacefully avoided by Radoslav's retirement to the monastery as a monk. The Latin King of Constantinople, although hostile to the Orthodox Kingdom of Serbia, was no longer a danger. Nor was the Bulgarian King Asen a danger because of Vladislav's marriage to the Bulgarian princess. On the other hand, the Serbian national Church was well organized, monasteries were working in full sway with spiritual and missionary activities, and the religious and moral level of the people had been raised. Enumerating all these achievements, Sava of course did not say whose they were, but Vladislav knew it without being told. Therefore, concluded Sava, his presence was no longer indispensable, and he might be of much greater use to his country from the outside. So ended the conversation of the archbishop and the king. After his interview with the king ended, Sava gathered all the bishops and exhorted them with these words: "I beg you all to keep firmly all that you have seen and heard from me, that is, to look after your own lives first with repentance and improvement according to your faith in our Lord Jesus Christ, and then to teach the people confided to your care."

When the masses of people learned of Sava's intention to leave them forever, they cried with inconsolable grief: "O our good shepherd and teacher, Vladika Sava, do not leave us, your poor people alone, for who is like you to be in your place?" It was indeed a heartbreaking scene. And Sava, trying to console the weeping people, wept himself, just like a loving father parting from his beloved children.

During a hierarchical liturgy, Arsenije was consecrated by Archbishop Sava and the other bishops. The new archbishop was not unknown to the king and the people. He was especially respected and loved by all those masses of people who visited Žiča. They thought him an excellent successor to Sava. So when Sava announced him as the archbishop and installed him on his throne, the clergy and the people exclaimed: "To the Most Reverend Arsenije, the Archbishop of all the Serbian lands, long life!"

So the independent Serbian Church acquired her second archbishop, ordained in Serbia and by Serbian bishops. If Arsenije was not a second Sava, he certainly was the first and most illustrious archbishop to follow him in that office. And for thirty years to come he proved to be a worthy successor to Sava.

CHAPTER 38

THE SECOND PILGRIMAGE

To do good for the people in spite of their unworthiness has been the axiom of all apostles and saints. For the people, because of ignorance or false teaching, cannot easily discern between friend and foe or good and evil.

The Serbian people, however, were well aware of what Sava had been and what he had done for them, very often against their will. They loved him and felt that he loved them. The very poorest of the people remembered with pride and gratitude how the saint entered their huts and blessed them and their children with his hands and his gifts. He had taught them how to pray and work and educate their children, how to put their house in order and keep it clean, how to help each other individually or by group cooperation. No secular ruler would have done what he did willingly and joyfully. Indeed, the people felt that Sava's heart was a great heart, belonging to all, the beating of which produced a new power and a new joy which circulated through the individual hearts of all the nation. Therefore, the people were at a loss to understand why he was leaving them, making them orphans while he still was alive.

This question Sava answered with his Master's words, "It is better for you that I go away" (Jn 16:7). He did not go to Studenica for a rest, although he badly needed rest and peace after so many exhausting troubles. Nor did he go to the Holy Mountain, although he liked to live there more than anywhere else. He did not follow his own likes or dislikes; he had learned to steer his vessel according to God's will, as God's servant, as a temporary stranger on earth. Directed by God's Spirit, he planned to go to distant countries to work among foreign peoples for his Serbian people and for Orthodoxy as a whole. He had completed his work inside Serbia, now he wanted to continue and complete it abroad. The Serbian name, people and Church ought to be known to all nations of the world through their best and their saintliest ambassador. This was the directive that Sava had to follow.

As long as Sava's ship could be seen, a great number of people stood on the shore at Budva and bowed toward their dear saint, wailing and crying at his departure. Sava stood on the deck all the time, blessing with both hands his people and his country, until the ship had disappeared in a sudden fog, which had been sent by God in order to screen His saint and those with him from sea pirates. For the pirates, being informed by their spies of Sava's voyage, had gathered for an attack and for plunder. Sava's ship anchored safely at Brindisi in Italy. The bewildered pirates saw God's finger in this and came and fell at Sava's feet, confessing their sin and praying for forgiveness. Sava warned them to abstain in the future from their unlawful activities, gave them some gifts and blessed them. After the captain had provided the ship with necessities, they continued the long journey with sails set.

Now came a new disaster. Blasting winds shook the sea, the ship became a mere plaything of a roaring storm, and darkness covered the whole horizon. Gripped with deadly fear, the captain and all the voyagers asked Sava to pray to God. Sava readily obeyed. He asked his disciples to hold him upright because of the tottering ship, while he with hands lifted heavenward prayed: "O Lover of Man, do not despise the work of your hands. We are your work, have mercy upon us! Do not, O Lord, because of my sins drown all those with me. Let not the abyss of the sea be our common grave. But as you saved your disciples from the storm, even so save us today. For you are the same yesterday, today, and forever." Then he made the sign of the Cross and with a great voice cried, "In the name of our Lord and God Jesus Christ, I command you, ye winds and sea, be still!" And suddenly as if frightened by the holy name of Jesus Christ, the winds ceased and the sea calmed down. Then all the travelers aboard wanted to worship Sava. And while all asked his disciples about this man, his country and his people, praising him as an angel, Sava fled from them, and gave thanks to God.

When he arrived at Acre, Sava with his men went to St George's church, which he had bought back from the Latins and restored to the Monastery of St Sava the Sanctified. While he rested in that place, the captain, sailors and travelers spread the news in the city of their miraculous escape from death by the prayers of the Serbian saint. Hearing this, the chiefs of the city with a crowd of people came to see and greet Sava. They bowed before him, offered him the city's hospitality, and asked him for his prayers and blessings. Thus the name of Sava and the name of Serbia were honored for generations in that city of Acre.

In Jerusalem, Sava was again greeted by Patriarch Athanasius with brotherly cordiality as an old friend. The Serbs went first to the Holy Sepulcher of our Lord, to Golgotha and to the Church of the Resurrection. In all these places they worshiped our Lord Jesus Christ, who in these places had suffered and died for us and our sins in order to free us from the power of Satan, and finally had risen in glory as the true God.

The patriarch entertained Sava in his residence. The two hierarchs had long and intimate conversations, each eager to know more of the other's church and people. This time Sava stayed with his men on Zion in the Serbian Monastery of St John the Evangelist, which he had acquired during his first pilgrimage to Jerusalem.

Again a swarm of beggars and children, both Christian and Muslim, gathered around Sava. They remembered him from his first visit to the Holy City, his friendliness towards the poor and his liberality in almsgiving. Never before had a foreign prelate been so deeply honored by the lowly and the poor. They awaited him in the morning at the door of his monastery, they thronged around him in the streets, and they escorted him back home in the evening. They knew his name and they learned to know the name of his country and his people. They shouted: "Mar Saba, have mercy upon us!" Sava indeed had mercy upon them, giving them money, clothes and food in his monastery on the Mount of Zion, and praying for them to his Lord Jesus Christ.

Even long, long afterwards, whenever the populace of Jerusalem met a Serbian among the pilgrims, they asked him about "Mar Saba," praising him as a true man of God.

CHAPTER 39

AMONG FAITHFUL AND
INFIDEL

Nationalistic ideas, nationalist exclusion, cannot get us very far. We Christians cannot speak anymore of national religions or national deities. We have national churches, but definitely not national religions. Some people, even in our Christian era, confuse these two notions. In their chauvinistic zeal, they want to resuscitate the gods of their heathen ancestors, for a national religion cannot be other than heathen.

The first Serbian archbishop knew this very well. When he organized the Serbian national church, it was not from the idea of exciting chauvinism among Serbs and much less of resuscitating their pagan tribal religion. He only wanted, through the nationally organized church, to make his people a worthy member of the universal Orthodox family of Christ. He himself was permeated with the spirit of ecumenical Christianity. Thus he felt at home in every Orthodox community of every race and language.

From Jerusalem Sava went to Alexandria. The Patriarch of Alexandria, being well informed about the Archbishop of Serbia, his royal lineage, his austere life on the Holy Mountain, and his ordination by the Patriarch of Constantinople in Nicaea, received him with the cordiality of a brother. The more he conversed with Sava the more he respected and loved him. Sava recounted to the patriarch and his clergy the story of the Serbian people and the Church. They all listened with great interest, because it was new to them. On his part, the patriarch answered Sava's many questions about the apostolic Church of Alexandria, about her organization and practices. Meantime, Sava went to worship in the church of St. Mark, the apostle and founder of the Christian Church in that great city, also in the great church of St Menas, as well as in that of St Cyrus and

St John, the martyrs. In each one he left gifts and gave alms to the poor.

As he was in Alexandria, Sava wanted to visit the places where the great Fathers of the Desert lived. By reading their lives he had been encouraged as a young monk on his thorny path of monastic austerity by their astounding asceticism. The patriarch gladly fulfilled his wish and gave him experienced guides and interpreters. They traveled on camels through the sandy and pathless desert and visited the monasteries at the borders of Libya, and the Thebaid, Scetis and Nitria. Sava already knew from books the names of all the spiritual heroes in each of those places. In his prayers now he held conversations with them as with the living. He saw their tombs and entered their narrow cells or caves. Sava recalled them all: Paul, Anthony, Sisoes, Macarius, Pambo, Onuphrius, Paphnutius, Zeno, Pimen, Lot, Efrem, Arsenius and the whole army of Christ's soldiers. These strange soldiers fought not against men but against demons and fleshly desires, striving relentlessly for purity of heart which enabled them to see angels and spirits. Sava viewed and reviewed them with great admiration as spiritual athletes, who mocked the vanities of the world and were mocked by the world as "fools for Christ's sake." Yet in their "foolishness" they were often the desired teachers and advisers of kings and patriarchs. Patricians and princes from distant Gaul and Rome used to visit them and ask about God and the soul.

Sava contemplated the memory of those "earthly angels and heavenly men." In their half-ruined abodes, he still found some monks, hermits with whom he had long and hearty talks. They spoke Coptic or Arabic. They were praiseworthy men but were depressed because of frequent raids by the Muslims. He gave them gifts and asked for their prayers for the Serbian king, archbishop and people. Glad to have seen the lamp of ancient Light in the Desert still kept gleaming, he blessed those holy men and parted from them.

The caravan then proceeded to Cairo. Sava's arrival in the capital of the Muslim sultans created quite a sensation. The Muslims looked at the Christian monks and angrily asked: "Who are these infidels who so freely enter our city?" For the blood shed by the Crusaders had not yet dried. Sava realized that he was in great danger, but he relied upon God in constant silent prayer. Great Saladin, more humane than most of the Christian crusading princes, was dead. The new sultan, Saladin's relative, was more hostile toward the Christians. But when he was informed that Sava was the son of the great ruler and brother of kings, he issued an order that the distinguished visitor should be received with honor and, moreover, that food and all provisions for him and his companions should be sent every day from the sultan's palace to the Orthodox Metropolia, where Sava resided. The Muslim masses, seeing the unusual attention of their sultan toward Sava, changed their attitude. They began to gather around that extraordinary Christian dignitary, whom their sultan had honored more than any other Christian prelate. Soon they were captivated by Sava's friendly greetings and smiles and much more by his charity to the poor, especially to the blind, always very numerous in Egypt. The Metropolia was practically besieged by a mixed crowd of Christians and Muslims, both eager to get a glimpse of the Serbian saint, the Christians with satisfaction and the Muslims with admiration. The sultan rejoiced seeing how all his people shared his friendly feeling toward Sava. He ordered more provisions and gifts to be carried from his palace to the Metropolia. Also hearing that Sava wished to go outside of Cairo to visit some Christian holy places, the sultan gave him his guard. So Sava went to see the place where the Holy Virgin had lived with the boy Jesus and Joseph when they had settled in Egypt while escaping Herod's persecution. He also visited some Coptic churches and institutions and gave to each one rich donations.

Having returned to the city, Sava prepared to leave Egypt for

Mount Sinai. He had accomplished here what he had planned to do. By personal contact he had strengthened the regular cordial relations between the Serbian Church and the great Patriarchate of Alexandria. He made for his people new friends among the Muslims. He increased his own knowledge with new experiences in the desert as well as in the cities.

The sultan, hearing of Sava's intentions to leave, ordered his officers to accompany him to Mount Sinai itself. He presented Sava with many rare gifts, and Sava on his part lavishly gave money to the needy and to those who were of service to him.

Finally, Sava embraced his kind host, the Metropolitan, and gave blessings to his clergy and his people. A great crowd followed him, shouting greetings of farewell all the way until he mounted a camel.

After Sava's departure, the people in Egypt said of him, "Never has a more amiable Christian visited us than this man, who indeed is a true man of God."

CHAPTER 40

ON THE MOUNT OF
THE ANCIENT LAW

How difficult it has been for men and nations to believe in
one God! More difficult than to create great civilizations. The
superb civilizations of Egypt, Mesopotamia, Syria and Greece
had been darkened by the degrading worship of the forces of
nature, personified in many quarrelling divinities and expressed in stone and wooden idols. For two generations, Moses had
tried in the desert to educate the Israelites in the belief in one
God, and after forty years of hard efforts he died discontented.

Twenty-seven centuries later, there traveled through this
same desert the spiritual head of the Serbian Church, who had
dedicated his life to educate his own people, not only in the
belief in one God but in God Incarnate, the Messiah, whom
Moses had predicted.

It was very long and wearisome traveling through the hot,
waterless desert, with rare oases of water and palms. Sava's
caravan passed the pharaohs' mines of turquoise and
Solomon's mines of gold before it started climbing a steep and
rocky mountain. At a height of 5000 feet, a spiritual oasis came
into view. There was the Monastery of St Catherine, perched
like a swallow's nest on a much higher mount, Mount Sinai,
8,000 feet high. The monastery, still in existence, was encompassed by high walls and battlements and adorned by green
cypresses and poplar trees.

The Archbishop of Sinai, who was at the same time the
superior of the monastery, met the Serbian archbishop with
cordiality and joy. After a well-deserved rest, the Serbs went
into the Church of St Catherine. Then, taking their shoes off,
they proceeded to the Church of the Burning Bush, the very
spot from which God's angel spoke to Moses while he tended
the sheep of his father-in-law. "And lo the bush was burning,

yet was not consumed." And the angel said to him, "Moses, put off your shoes from your feet, for the place on which you are standing is holy ground" (Ex 3:2,5). Sava was very much moved and he frequently celebrated liturgy barefooted on this holy ground. He celebrated by turns in Greek and in Slavonic.

The monks of St Catherine eagerly listened to the stories of a very distant country called Serbia, recounted to them by their Serbian brother monks, the companions of Sava. They had never heard of such a country before, and now they became enthusiastic about the Serbs, their archbishop and their people. On their part they told their beloved guests the story of their monastery.

In the early days of Christianity, the hermits had settled in numerous caves on the slopes of the mountain. In the fourth century, Empress Helena built the first church over the site of the Burning Bush. Emperor Justinian built the great church to the memory of St Catherine, and also the great walls for protection against Bedouins. In time this place became the beacon of Christendom, famous on account of its many spiritual athletes, theologians and martyrs. Now from Sava's lips the monks heard mentioned the names, writings and deeds of a great number of those who had made that Mount well known and respected all over the Christian world. The names of St John of the Ladder, St Nilus with his son Theodulos, Akakius, George, Anastasius and others were as familiar to Sava as to them. The monks were extremely impressed by the vast knowledge of the Serbian archbishop as well as by his wonderful loving kindness and his humility.

The superior showed Sava the famous library, as well as many relics and other priceless treasures donated to the monastery by kings and commoners from all over the world, and preserved there for many centuries. He took Sava to the top of Mount Sinai, where Moses had received from God the two tables of the Ancient Law with the Ten Commandments. It lies 3000 feet above the site of the Burning Bush. To get to the top, one needs to climb 3500 steps. There in a thundering voice God spoke to Moses: "I am the Lord your God," and also: "I am, who I am." Later on, however, the Lord spoke at that same place to the Prophet Elijah "in a small voice" (Ex 3:14; I Kgs 19:11-12). God's ways are manifold.

Sava stayed at the monastery on Sinai over two months. During Lent he celebrated the Holy Eucharist at the altars within the monastery, and every Saturday he would climb to the top of Horeb, the highest peak, in order to spend whole nights in vigil there. Early on Sundays he descended to the monastery for liturgy.

On Easter, both archbishops celebrated solemn services in St Catherine's, and then the Serbs prepared to move on. Sava gave a large sum of money to the monastery for remembrance in daily prayer of the Serbian people and their leaders, and he also received some gifts from the superior. Then he took leave of his hosts. The bonds of mutual knowledge, respect and love made by Sava's visit to this holy place had linked Sava forever with the Church of Sinai. In the course of time, some Serbian monks lived in the brotherhood of Sinai, and the Sinaites visited Serbia and even had a monastery of their own in Toplica.

Now Sava turned his face again to Jerusalem. In those days people seldom dared to undertake pilgrimages to such a distant places as Mount Sinai, for traveling was insecure and roads beset with many dangers. For this reason Sava was admired all the more by the clergy and the people of Jerusalem on his return. Multitudes hurried to see and greet those daring Serbs and their spiritual leaders. Even in the Church of the Resurrection, the patriarch on this account spoke enthusiastically of the Serbs. At a solemn service in front of the Holy Sepulcher, the patriarch, as though inspired from above, prophetically said of Sava and his people: "These are new Apostles, who were hitherto hidden by the Lord. These are the fulfillers of the Gospel of Christ. These are the new martyrs, the bearers of the

Cross and the sufferings of the lord, and in spite of that they have followed Him faithfully and joyfully. They are shedding their blood and laying down their lives for His sake." So the holy Patriarch Athanasius foretold the glory and the martyrdom of Sava's people in centuries and generations to come.

Again crowds of people followed Sava wherever he moved in the streets of the Holy City, greeting him as an old friend. Again Sava with benevolence and smiles distributed charity to them. Then he could not resist his wish to go once more the Monastery of Mar Saba. He had particularly close ties with this monastery, he and through him his people forever. For many centuries since, that monastery was never without Serbian monks in its brotherhood. Having returned to Jerusalem, Sava amazed Patriarch Athanasius by telling him of his plans to go to Babylon, a still longer and more dangerous journey than to Sinai. "This man," said the patriarch, looking at Sava, aged and exhausted, "seems to seek martyrdom and death." They blessed each other with tears of affection and so parted.

CHAPTER 41

A HAZARDOUS JOURNEY

A caravan from Jerusalem normally took 30 days to reach Bagdad if all went well. Without shrinking before the many dangers ahead, the sandy desert, scorching heat and bandits, Sava undertook this voyage. Relying upon God's protection, he reached the fabulous city on the Tigris River without any grave occurrence. The Muslim population there was hostile to the Christians even more than that in Egypt. Yet the Sultan of Iraq received Sava with tolerance and even with respect, gave him a great house for his temporary abode and a guard for protection.

Sava proceeded at once to the Church of the Three Young Men: Shadrach, Meshach and Abednego. The wonderful story of these three is recounted in the Book of Daniel. In Bagdad, there lived a small minority of Christians, Assyro-Chaldeans, whose forefathers had accepted the blessed faith in the first century through the Apostle Thaddeus. They are courageous people whose whole history even up to our day has been one of sheer martyrdom. Although they were not quite Orthodox in some aspects of their faith, Sava sympathized with them because they clung stubbornly to Christ amid many deadly dangers. He had a friendly conversation with their patriarch and the elders of the community. He left his donation to the church and went to visit the ruins of some of the Christian sanctuaries.

There was not much reason for our saint to tarry long in Bagdad, "the abode of peace," the famous capital of Harun-Al-Rashid, the commander of the faithful and the chief hero of the Arabian Nights. Its great glory belonged to the past and the dreams of the living. Yet it still existed as a big if not a glorious city, whereas Babylon and Nineveh had perished without leav-

140

ing even a trace of their existence.

Once on the soil of Syria, Sava vividly recalled the personalities of the great apostles who had established and organized the church in that country and also all the celebrated Orthodox teachers, bishops and ascetics. For though he himself was an ascetic, he was also a man of refined culture and great knowledge. He knew how Syria had been for centuries a spiritual battlefield, first between Christianity and paganism, then between Christianity and heresy, and lastly between Christianity and Islam.

The city of Antioch was the apostolic see, where the followers of Christ for the first time were called "Christians." Arriving in this city, Sava went to pay homage to the apostolic successor, the Patriarch of Antioch and all Syria. The patriarch already knew of the Serbian archbishop from hearsay and from correspondence with his colleagues, the patriarchs of the East. So he received Sava with keen interest. After the first conversation he found his visitor very much to his liking. Many days they prayed and talked together, both of them eager to learn from each other. Sava visited the Monastery of St Simeon the Stylite, where the monks received him with enthusiasm as an Athonite monk and as the head of a newly organized independent Church. Sava was eager to know more of St Simeon and his successors in that place, and the brothers satisfied his wish. He gave a donation to the monastery and blessings to the monks. He also offered gifts to the cathedral in Antioch, and the patriarch in turn presented him with some valuable relics and church vessels. At the end, Sava and the patriarch gave each other their blessings and thus separated.

From Syria, Sava ventured to go to Armenia, the country at the foot of Ararat. He wished very much to see the martyred nation with a rich church history, and the spiritual children of St Gregory the Illuminator. As usual, he paid a visit both to the living and to the dead. He knew by name many departed holy Armenian bishops, Christian princes and martyrs. It was in that country also that St John Chrysostom had met his death in exile in 407. Sava conversed with all of them in his prayers and meditations. He visited the celebrated monasteries of ancient Armenia, presented them with gifts and listed the names of many Serbs, living and dead, to be prayed for.

Now leaving Armenia, Sava had before him the most dangerous trip of all. He had to cross Kurdistan, a wild mountainous country, inhabited by a fierce people, the Kurds, who had been responsible for many massacres of Christians, Armenians and Assyrians. It might have been of some help that Sava was acquainted with the Egyptian sultan, who was of the Kurd dynasty, founded by Saladin, the most prominent man in the history of Kurdistan. Yet a better explanation was presented by a biographer who wrote: "Like lightning, armed with the Holy Spirit, adorned with God's grace, Sava tread upon serpents and scorpions, and over all the power of the enemy' (Lk 10:19)."

Then Sava traveled through Seljuk-Turkey, a country no less hostile to Christians than Kurdistan. On his way he saw with sadness that many Christian churches had been turned into mosques with minarets. He could hardly foresee that at a distant time many of the Serbian churches he or his father had built would suffer the same fate. He generously showered his money upon the poor Muslims in every town and village. And he could not have foreseen at the time that their descendants would drag away innumerable Serbian slaves and sell them in the markets in those very places where he now spread charity in Christ's name.

Arriving safely at a port on the Mediterranean, the Serbs sailed aboard a ship to Nicaea. There Sava was received as an old friend with even greater solemnity and cordiality than ever before by the imperial court, the patriarch and the Christian people. They all listened to his stories of the remotest holy places of the east. He presented the emperor, John Vatatzes, the empress and the patriarch with precious ikons and other sacred objects brought from his pilgrimage. He preached in the churches and gave charity to the poor. Moreover, he successfully urged the emperor and patriarch to recognize the Bulgarian Patriarch of Trnovo for the sake of the unity and strength of Orthodoxy. He also pleaded that King Asen, who had previously turned to the Roman Church and lately abjured his error, should be forgiven.

This was Sava's third visit to the temporary capital of the Byzantine emperor and the patriarch. The unusual impression he made upon the people of Nicaea remained ineradicable as long as the Christians lived in that city. The tie between the Serbian Church and the Mother Church was to last.

From Nicaea Sava could not go through the Bosphorus to Constantinople. The Latins still held that city and, besides, it was besieged just at the time by the army of Emperor John Vatatzes of Nicaea. Therefore, the emperor arranged Sava's trip cautiously along the Asian coast of the Bosphorus, northward to a little port, from which the Serbs crossed the Black Sea and landed in the town of Mesembria in Bulgaria.

CHAPTER 42

THE END OF PILGRIMAGE AND OF LIFE

There is a proverb of the Serbs: "Work as if expecting to live a hundred years, and pray as if expecting to die tomorrow." Another is: "There is no death but on the destined day."

Both of these proverbs could be applied to the life of St Sava. The more he advanced in age, the more he worked, vigilantly expecting death. He seemed to some people to be indomitable. He himself, however, was deeply convinced that this death did not depend on the manifold dangers through which he passed, but on God's will.

The dangers for Sava, however, were not yet over. From the town of Mesembria he could see the high range of the Balkan mountains, all covered with deep snow and frost. He had to pass over it, and it was early December. When King Asen learned of Sava's landing in Bulgaria, he quickly sent his chief of staff with servants and horses to help the Serbs over the frosty ridges and precipices of the Balkans and to bring them to Trnovo, his royal capital.

Riding on horseback for several days through Bulgaria, Sava plunged into meditations on God's providence. He was wondering whether the Lord, who had fulfilled all his heart's desires throughout life, would fulfill his last desire, which was to die in a foreign country. Now Bulgaria was the last foreign country he was to traverse. He dreaded God's reluctance in responding to his desire. Yet he quickly drove away his dread and recovered full confidence in God. He had good reason to rejoice that he had reached Bulgaria alive because of the good news he was bringing to the king and the patriarch from Nicaea.

When the Serbian pilgrims entered Great Trnovo, King Asen came out with his court and met Sava with evident joy and honor. He took him " to his warm palace because it happened to be bitterly cold."

After a short rest, Sava had long talks with King Asen and Patriarch Joachim. He told them what he had done for them in Nicaea. "The Bulgarian Patriarchate has been recognized and Asen forgiven and blessed," he said. After his congratulations to both of his hosts, Sava opened his bags and presented the king and the patriarch with priceless gifts brought from the East. His bags were filled with golden vessels and service books, embroidered vestments and curtains, lamps and crosses, candlesticks, censers, staffs, and boxes with saints' relics adorned with precious stones and pearls, all shining with oriental beauty. Sava gave a part of it to the Bulgarian king and the patriarch and retained an ample portion for the churches in Serbia, for King Vladislav and Archbishop Arsenije. Both Asen and Joachim were exceedingly grateful to their guest, first because of the reconciliation he had brought about between them and Nicaea and then also for the wonderful gifts he had brought for them and for the Bulgarian churches. Above all they were captivated by the charm of Sava's holy personality. Just like a father to his children, he had brought to the Bulgarians great gifts from far-off countries, and as a saint he had filled with holiness their souls, their city and their country.

King Asen made great feasts in Sava's honor. But all those worldly feasts could not dim the heavenly light in the soul of the saint. Like the psalmist, he desired one thing above all, which was "to dwell in the House of the Lord all the days of my life, to behold the beauty of the Lord" (Ps 27:4). Therefore, he went to the church services every day, mostly to the new Church of the Forty Martyrs, founded by King Asen. He celebrated liturgy several times between Christmas and Epiphany. He preached at every service. He blessed the Bulgarian people just as if they were his own.

According to the wish of the king and patriarch, Sava blessed the water on the eve of Epiphany and sprinkled the king and the people with it. Also on the day of Epiphany he celebrated the Eucharist together with Patriarch Joachim, the Serbian and Bulgarian clergy assisting.

Now King Asen, though a passionate hunter, abstained from going hunting between Christmas and Epiphany, delighting more in conversations with Sava than in anything else. But after Epiphany, he asked his eminent guest not to be in a hurry to go home, but "wait, holy Vladika," said he, "for the end of this biting winter, and restfully abide with us in thine own house until Easter." Saying this, the King kissed Sava's hands and went off to hunt.

In the evening of that same day of Epiphany, Sava felt fever in his body. On the following day, the fever increased. At once he became aware of approaching death. But instead of being sad or alarmed, he quickly set to work, to do what was yet undone. Now the minutes were like days for him, and days years. He called some of his disciples and gave them all the bags and trunks with the precious gifts destined for Serbia. He wrote a letter to King Vladislav and another to Archbishop Arsenije. And after blessing those disciples, his faithful companions, he sent them to Serbia. They went lamenting, alone without their beloved father. After that, he collected all the money he had left and gave it to be distributed to the needy in Trnovo. He handed to his disciples his personal garments and belongings, some for themselves and some for Archbishop Arsenije. And although he had written letters to the King and the Archbishop of Serbia, he gave oral orders and instructions to the disciples concerning ecclesiastical matters. He entrusted to them some of his written notes on various religious customs and practices as well as on the cultural and social life of different peoples and at royal courts in the East. He recommended to his countrymen to accept what was the best and noblest.

Patriarch Joachim was much disturbed by Sava's illness, all the more so since he had heard Sava saying that he was going to die soon. He suggested that the king should be informed, but

Sava disagreed. Finally, the dying saint expressed hearty thanks to the patriarch for his attendance and asked him to leave him alone. Joachim embraced Sava and went out in a fit of weeping. Only the Serbian monks, like shadows in a corner of the room, kept the watch over their beloved father. Sava prayed:

"O Lord of my father, how great is Thy power, how sweet Thy love.

"Immeasurable have been Thy mercies upon me; how can I measure Thy mercies upon all Thy creatures?

"Verily, there is no darkness for Thine eyes, no perplexity for Thy wisdom, no comparison with Thy holy beauty.

"Thou hast guided me from my youth with Thy right hand, and nourished me with the milk and honey of Thy wisdom.

"I have been only Thy tool in shepherding one of Thy peoples toward Thy heavenly fold.

"O Mercifiul Lord, bless the people of my father Saint Simeon, and make them great in holiness among nations.

"I worship Thee, I praise Thee, O my Lord, for Thou hast fulfilled also my last desire to die in a foreign land; forgive me my doubts.

"All the goods received from Thee I have given to others, and now the last one, my soul, I return to Thy hands.

"Be merciful to my sinful soul, O Christ my Lord, and take it to the abode of my father Simeon, through the intercessions of Thy Holy Mother Virgin Mary and all Thy saints."

Thereafter, Sava took Holy Communion and then still continued to pray, in a whispering voice, for many persons and nations by name, and for those he had known in the past, and for those unknown to him in the future.

Then at dawn of the following day, January 14, 1235, the watching disciples heard a mysterious voice say:

"Rejoice, my servant, lover of truth!" And a little later again:

"Come, my good and faithful servant, receive the rewards

which I have promised to all who love me."

At that moment, Sava smiled with joy, and gave up his holy soul to God. The disciples quickly put a burning candle at his head according to an ancient custom, and crossed his hands over his breast. Such was the separation from the body of a soul destined for immortal life and glory.

CHAPTER 43

THE ORTHODOX WORLD
IN MOURNING

The death of a member of a family is a blow to that family.
The death of a king or a national hero is a blow to his nation.
But the death of a saint is a blow to many nations and even to
the world. For a true saint is like heavenly fresh air to weaker
human souls. Besides, there is a popular belief in the East that
the death of a holy man is God's punishment of a people, or a
sign of approaching punishment.

Sava's death was mourned wherever people knew him or had
heard of him, East or West, from Hungary to Mount Sinai, but
nowhere so much as in Serbia and Bulgaria.

The dead body of Sava was buried on the day following his
death, as is usual in the Balkans up to our day. It was buried in
King Asen's Church of the Forty Martyrs according to the wish
of the King. Hearing of Sava's death, the king was desolate. He
was angry with Patriarch Joachim for not having informed him
of the archbishop's illness. He came too late for the burial. The
body of the deceased was taken in a procession from the royal
palace to the church. And what a marvelous procession
through many streets of the city before they came to the
church! After a solemn requiem and a long parade of wailing
people, Sava's body was laid in a tomb.

On his return, King Asen at once proceeded to his church to
pray at the tomb of the saint. His sorrow was very deep,
mitigated only by his satisfaction that the body of such a saint
should repose in his new church as a holy adornment of it. He
made a sarcophagus of one solid stone for Sava's body, and
adorned it with a golden lamp over it, and two precious
candlesticks on both sides of it. Moreover, he covered the sarcophagus with his own royal purple. He did so much for Sava's
continual memory that the Bulgarian people were touched by

149

their king's love toward this saint.

Let us now return to Serbia. Apart from a letter which Sava had written from Jerusalem to Archimandrite Spiridon of Studenica, there is no trace of his correspondence with Serbia during the eighteen months of his pilgrimage until his disciples brought his last letters to King Vladislav and Archbishop Aresenije. We do not know the contents of those letters. In them Sava must have announced his approaching death in a foreign country. Most probably those last letters were Sava's last will, his testament to the Serbian people. The king and the archbishop kept the sad news of Sava's illness for themselves as they still had some hope. But soon afterwards, a second party of Sava's companions arrived with still sadder news, that of his death.

This news produced consternation and deep mourning throughout the Serbian countryside, from the royal palace to the shepherds' huts. And since the people's sorrows did not subside for a long time, Archbishop Arsenije said to King Vladislav: "It is neither meet nor right before God and men to let the body of our father remain outside of his native country and away from his church and his people in a foreign land. You know yourself how he has been God's priceless gift to us. He has been equal to the apostles. He has undergone many toils, strains and sufferings for the sake of our Serbian people. He has sanctified our land with many new churches, established a kingdom with an archbishopric and many bishoprics. He has created institutions, restored order and laid out a lawful and Godlike course of life. Therefore, do all within your power to bring him over here to his own fatherland."

King Vladislav readily accepted the archbishop's wise advice. He had another reason to follow this advice, however. The masses of the people, with a number of noblemen, charged him with responsibility for making Sava leave Serbia. Vladislav had saddened the saint by making disorder in the royal family through the overthrow of King Radoslav. Consequently, the people's ill will toward Vladislav was increased by Sava's death in a foreign country, and the dissatisfaction grew louder and louder.

Therefore, King Vladislav wrote a letter to King Asen, his father-in-law, asking him to allow Sava's body to be transferred to Serbia. He sent this letter by an officer of high rank.

CHAPTER 44

FROM TRNOVO TO MILEŠEVO

The transfer of saints' relics after death is a striking feature of the Christian Church. The common reason for this is the desire of every land to possess a saint's body or relics for its well-being and blessing. A special reason for the removal of saints' bodies in the Christian East and the Balkans had been the Muslim invasion. Many of the Serbian saints were moved from one country to another or from one place to another. The body of St Stefan the First-Crowned, which now lies in Studenica, was moved fourteen times.

St Sava was no exception. His body was claimed by both Bulgaria and by Serbia, each with good reason. King Asen refused to give up Sava's body, explaining in his answer to King Vladislav: "If the body of the saint were among us without due attention and honor, you would be perfectly right in asking that it be taken from us in order that you might keep it with greater care and honor. But since the saint, by God's providence, died in our country, and since his sacred body, greatly honored by us, reposes in a church of God, why then do you trouble him and us by your request?"

Receiving this negative answer, the Serbian king became very sorrowful. He therefore wrote another letter to the King of Bulgaria, and sent several more men of high rank to support his demand orally. In this second letter, he implored his father-in-law, saying, "If I have found any grace before you, my father, do not close your heart toward me. Give me the sacred body of my uncle and my lord."

Moved by this second letter, King Asen was at a loss as to what to do. Therefore, he called the Council of State with Patriarch Joachim and put the matter before them for decision. They all decidedly stood against the wish of the Serbian

King. "The people in the city would rebel if they heard of it," said the councilors and the patriarch. "Then," they added, "the church you founded, deprived of Sava's sacred relics, will be impoverished and degraded. The people, disappointed, will cease to crowd your church as they are doing now on account of the saint's body in it. Therefore, we are all against the removal of his body."

Accepting the decision of his councilors, Asen wrote back to Vladislav: "Since it has been the will of God that the saint should die amongst us, and we are Christ's faithful too, who am I to oppose the will of God? And how can I dare disturb the tomb of the saint, especially as he himself did not say a word about the transfer of his body to Serbia? Therefore, my son, ask from me whatever else you want, but do not force me to do what I cannot easily do. For the patriarch and all my councilors and all my people forbid me to do it."

This letter is remarkable as a testimony of the extraordinary respect the Bulgarian people had for St Sava. But it made Vladislav desperate and frightened too. For the people already knew about this correspondence, and they wanted by all means Sava's body sent back to Serbia. If the King failed in bringing it home, the people would interpret it as Sava's own displeasure with his nephew even after death. And what then? Vladislav would lose his throne.

Finally, King Vladislav decided to go himself to Trnovo. And he went with a solemn escort of noblemen and bishops and with rich gifts. He was received in the Bulgarian capital with real paternal love by his father-in-law and with a formal display of royal magnificence. But his mind was preoccupied more with his dead uncle than with all the living and swarming crowd around him, for his fate depended more on the great dead than on all the living. Therefore, he proceeded at once to the Church of the Forty Martyrs, prostrated himself at the tomb of St Sava and prayed with tears: "I know, my father, that my sin prompted you to leave Serbia, and even caused your death in a foreign country. But forgive me for the love of your brother and my father. Forsake not your people for whom you have undergone so many troubles and pains, and clothe me not with shame and misery. Pray to God and by your prayers move the heart of King Asen to give me your body, lest I be scorned by my people if I return without you."

This and many similar prayers Vladislav offered with a contrite heart to his uncle, and not without effect. For on that same night, King Asen had a dream which disturbed him very much. Sava appeared to him in the dream and commanded him as from God to give his body to the Serbs. On the morrow, Asen assembled his Council and told them of his dream. It struck all the councilors with dread, most of all Patriarch Joachim. But after some discussion, they finally agreed that the body should be given, lest God's punishment befall them.

Accordingly, the coffin was taken out of the sarcophagus and opened in the presence of the two kings, the patriarch, the clergy and a mass of people. To their joy, Sava's body was found whole and incorrupt and a pleasant scent emanated from it as if he were sleeping. Suddenly, wonders occurred: the sick were instantly healed and demoniacs cleansed by the mere touch of his body or robes. The news of those miraculous healings was quickly spread in the city, and masses of people thronged to the church to see and to touch the new saint. The patriarch ordered that the church should stay open day and night for the people and their invalids. King Asen on his part ordered that the stone sarcophagus should be kept in honor just as if the sacred body was still lying in it. The royal purple should cover the sarcophagus, the lamp and candles around it burn continually, just as before.

Thereupon King Asen made a great feast at the royal court in honor of his son-in-law. In his toast at that feast, Asen said to Vladislav: "I wished to have this saint in my church as God's gift. Therefore I adorned his tomb as you have seen. But because your royal Highness has taken the trouble to come in person to see me as to your father, I will not, my son, let you return sorrowful. You have indeed snatched from me the saint, my God-given treasure. Let your heart rejoice now. And we hope too to receive God's mercy through his intercessions, because we have had great love for him during his life and after his death." Hearing this, King Vladislav with all his Serbian companions got up from the table, bowed deeply before King Asen and thanked him most heartily.

We have mentioned before how King Asen asked Sava to stay in Trnovo until Easter "as in your own house." Sava did not promise to stay, but he stayed after his death in Bulgaria, over two Eastertides. And now it was the beautiful spring season, after the second Easter, when Sava's body was taken from Trnovo and brought over the Bulgarian frontier to Serbia. What frontier? There was no fixed frontier between the Serbs and the Bulgars, but always a fluctuating one, no real boundary between two different nations. Saint Sava has been and has always remained the symbol of this unity. The Serbs were sad because he was away from them, and the Bulgarian rejoiced in having him. Now the feelings were reversed; the Serbs rejoiced in getting him back, and the Bulgarians became sad in parting from him. In all the villages and towns through which the Serbian group went with Sava's body, the Bulgarian people rushed in crowds to bow before that body, to touch it, to kiss it and to honor it. The same thing happened on Serbian soil. Archbishop Arsenije with numerous clergy, state dignitaries and an immense mass of people met the body of the saint.

In Serbian history, there is no record of such a long and solemn procession as that in which the body of St Sava was taken from Bulgaria to Serbia. Thousands upon thousands of people rushed from everywhere to take part in that procession. With psalms, songs, canticles and prayers, the procession went on, but it was slowed by the masses of people in every town and village who blocked it and held it for a while in order to see, touch or kiss their saint.

King Vladislav had built a church in Hercegovina, called Mileševo. After seven hundred years it is still a wonderful church; it could easily be the adornment of any big city. How wonderful it must have been in those days is hard to imagine. He dedicated Mileševo to God, Pantocrator, like Žiča. Apart from all his other virtues and mistakes, his foundation church shows that he was a great Christian. His fresco-portrait in the church represents him as a man with blue eyes and short beard, kind and charitable. As a sign of reconciliation between his uncle and himself, Vladislav purposely brought Sava's body to his church of Mileševo to be buried there.

It had been over half a century since Prince Rastko left Hercegovina and had fled to the Holy Mountain. And now he had been brought back as Saint Sava to that same province, Hercegovina.

The father had returned to his children. His tomb in Mileševo became the source of grace, health and consolation for Serbian generations to come. Nobody ever believed he was dead.

CHAPTER 45

IN THE FLAME OF THE PYRE

The Turkish conquest of the Balkans included Serbia, too. The Serbs resisted longer than any other Balkan nation. Smederevo, the last capital of a reduced Serbia, fell in 1459, six years after Constantinople. Montenegro alone remained unconquered. The Turkish rule put an end to national states and dynasties and to human liberty, progress and prosperity in the Balkan nations. The Church became the only source of strength and solace left to Christians, but they had to pay the oppressors a terrible price in blood. Some of the finest churches were turned into mosques, many others destroyed, and all were looted and spoiled. Žiča was half ruined and devasted.

Mileševo was plundered and disfigured, but happily not destroyed. The sarcophagus with Sava's incorruptible body was not removed or desecrated for one hundred and fifty years after the Turkish conquest. Ever since Sava's body was laid in it, and for over two hundred years of Serbian freedom and independence, Mileševo had been a place for pilgrimages, equal to Žiča and Studenica. It had been endowed and adorned by the Bans of Bosnia, the Princes of Hercegovina, the Župans of the seacoast and kings and tsars of Serbia. The petty lords wanted to make themselves great, and the great would make themselves still greater if they had some connection with Sava's tomb or Sava's name. So Tvrtko I chose Mileševo in which to be crowned King of Bosnia at the tomb of St Sava in 1377, although he was a protector of the Bogomils. Prince Stjepan Kossača, an open Bogomil, adopted the title "Duke of St Sava." Of course, the Orthodox rulers competed even more eagerly with each other to do something remarkable for that sanctuary in which the sacred body was preserved. In those bright days of freedom, Mileševo was a true center of lofty

157

piety, education and educational activity. For Sava's spirit ruled there and gave an example of strenuous labor and many accomplishments.

In the dark days of Turkish tyranny, however, Mileševo became to the Christian people a place of retreat, of deep repentance and of heavenly consolation. It was at the mercy of the Muslims and yet, strange as it may seem, it was for a long time protected by the Muslims themselves and the Serbs who were converted by force to Islam. The Muslims also witnessed innumerable miracles at the tomb of Saint Sava. A large village of Muslim converts, Hissarjik, close to the monastery, surpassed all others in their devotion to and protection of Mileševo. Some of the daring European travelers who came to Serbia under the Osmanlis saw in Mileševo the sarcophagus of Saint Sava "heaped with the gifts given by the Muslims." Some of them mentioned that even Roman Catholics from Dalmatia and Jews made pilgrimages to the tomb of the saint.

This situation lasted until the end of the sixteenth century. But in that century the Osmanli Turks became exasperated because of the ceaseless revolts and insurrections of the Serbs. The Serbs had never reconciled themselves to their cruel fate under the Turkish yoke. Guerrillas from forests inside the country on the one hand, and refugees from Srem, Slavonia and Banat on the other, constantly disturbed the Ottoman government. The Turks thought the trouble makers and revolutionist had been inspired by the ancient Serbians monasteries. The cult and veneration of Saint Sava was then as great as ever before, and even greater on account of increasingly accumulated wonders.

Facing the growing danger of frequent insurrection, the Turkish sultans of that time were imprudent enough to use means contrary to wisdom. Instead of dousing fire by water, they intensified it by wood and straw. They sent more and more petty tyrants to suppress the revolts by torture, destruction and bloodshed.

At the beginning of the year 1595, a change took place on the throne in Istanbul. The new sultan, Mohamed III, son of a weak father, cruelly ordered Sinan Pasha to quell the Serbian revolts forever by any means. This ruthless pasha was informed that the Serbian monasteries were inspirational centers for all the revolts against the Turks. He was informed that Mileševo was a place of pilgrimage, a new Kaba, even for Muslims, and that many of them had been converted to the Christian faith because of the healing of their sick relations, and other wonders at the tomb of Saint Sava. Sinan Pasha at once ordered that Sava's body be taken to Belgrade and burnt.

A certain Ahmed beg Ochuse was assigned the commission to carry out the pasha's order. This brutal servant of the brutal lord, true to his nature, did it in a brutal way. He first placed a military cordon around the monastery of Mileševo. Then he forced the monks to take the wooden coffin with the body of the saint out of the sarcophagus. The coffin was put on horses which were led by the monks themselves, because the Turks were afraid to touch it. And so the melancholy procession started. On the way the sobbing and crying monks were beaten and every Serbian man or woman met on the way was killed or taken along, lest they should inform the outlaws in the forests. So in this way the procession swelled considerably by the time it reached Belgrade.

In the outskirts of the city of Belgrade, at a place called Vračar, a pyre was made. On that pyre the wooden coffin containing the sacred body was laid. On April 27, 1595, Saint Sava's body was burnt to ashes. An unusually big flame soared heavenward, illuminated the city in the night and was seen from over the Danube River. And while the Turks were celebrating with satisfaction, and the enslaved Serbs in Belgrade were weeping and praying, the free Serbs beyond the Danube and the guerrillas on the mountains presented their swords in homage to their saint.

So Sinan Pasha destroyed the body of Saint Sava, but increased his glory and influence. The triumph was only passing because it destroyed a cage from which the dove had fled long ago. The joy of the Turks was of short duration, for as the flame subsided, a sudden fear seized them, and they ran to their homes and shut the doors behind them. In Vracar a few monks on their knees watched the fire from afar, waiting to take a handful of sacred ashes back to Mileševo.

The living soul of the saint, however, looked triumphantly at the fire from the invisible world. For Sava's lifelong desire to be also a martyr for Christ's sake was now fulfilled. Therefore, with the smile of a victor, Sava forgave Sinan Pasha, and blessed his Serbian people.

With the Lord on my side I do not fear.

What can man do to me?

(Ps 118:6)

BIBLIOGRAPHY

BAŠIĆ, MILIVOJE. *Stare srpske biografije.* Beograd, 1924.

ĆOROVIĆ, VLADIMIR. *Sv. Sava u narodnom predanju.* Beograd, 1927.

DMITRIJEVIĆ, STEVAN. *Sv. Sava u narodnom verovanju i predanju.* Beograd, 1926.

DOMENTIJAN. *Životi Sv. Save i Sv. Simeona.* Beograd, 1938.

DUČIĆ, NIĆIFOR. *Istorija srpske pravoslavne crkve.* Beograd, 1894.

GIBBON, EDWARD. *History of the Decline and Fall of the Roman Empire.* Boston, 1856.

GRUIĆ, R. *Srpska pravoslavna crkva.* Beograd, 1920.

JIREČEK, KONSTANTIN. *Istorija Srba. I-a knjiga.* Beograd, 1922.

---- Istorija Bugara.

LAFFAN, R.G.D. *The Guardians of the Gates. Historial Lectures on the Serbs.* Oxford, 1918.

LANE-POOL, STANLEY. *Turkey,* London, 1888.

MARKOVIĆ, VASILIJE. *Pravoslavno monavštvo.* Beograd, 1920.

NOVAKOVIĆ, STOJAN. *Zakonski spomenici srpskih dřzava.* Beograd, 1912.

OBOLENSKY, DMITRY. *The Bogomils.* Cambridge, 1948.

OMAN, C.W. *The Byzantine Empire.* London, 1892.

PATERIK ATHONSKI.

PETKOVIC, VLADIMIR. *Studenica.* Beograd, n.d.

RADONIC, JOVAN. *Sveti Sava i njegovo doba.* Sremski karlovci, 1935.

ŠAFAŘIK, PAVEL JOSEF. *Památky dřevniho pisemnictvi' Jihoslovanou,* Praze, 1873.

SNEGAROV, IVAN. *Historia na Ochridskata Archiepiskopia. I tome. Sofia, 1924.*

STANOJEVIC, STANOJE. *Sveti Sava.* Beograd, 1935.

VASIĆ, MILIVOJE. *Žicǎ i Lazarica.* Beograd, 1928.

VELIMIROVICH, BISHOP NIKOLAJ D. *Serbian Orthodox Church.* London, 1917.